MacArthur Middle School

ON YOUR BICYCLE

ON YOUR BICYCLE

An illustrated history of cycling

James McGurn

Facts On File Publications
New York, New York • Oxford, England

Copyright © 1987 James McGurn
First published in the United States of America by Facts on File, Inc. 460 Park
Avenue South, New York, New York 10016

Library of Congress Cataloguing-in-Publication Data

McGurn, James, 1953–
    On your bicycle.

    British ed. published under title: On your bicycle.
    Bibliography: p.
    Includes index.
    1. Bicycles—History.   I. Title.
TL400.M37   1987   629.2'272'09   87–8959
ISBN 0–8160–1748–4

Printed in Great Britain

10 9 8 7 6 5 4 3 2 1

CONTENTS

ACKNOWLEDGEMENTS

I am grateful to the following for their guidance and criticisms: Bill Bush, Bob French, Philip and Pam Ingerson, Alan Leng, Hugh MacPherson, Augusto Marinoni, Avner Offer, Bob Poole, Peter Shirtcliffe, Helen Sinclair, Jim Spriggs, Roger Street, Aad Streng, Mike West and Nancy Woodhead. Alan Leng of the Cyclists' Touring Club gave me unlimited access to the Club's archives and trusted me with some valuable old photographs. Martin Ayres of *Cycling* let me look at his magazine's archives and kindly furnished illustrations. I also used the library of the Southern Veteran-Cycle Club and have benefitted greatly from the knowledge and scholarship of numerous fellow-members, and of Derek Roberts in particular. The pioneering work of Andrew Ritchie has been a great inspiration. I thank Roger Hudson for his excellent guidance, and John Worrallo for his inestimable photographic services. In the course of my researches I was constantly aware of the value of the British public library system, and I am especially indebted to the staff of York City Library.

To Sally, Matthew, Richard,
Kenny and Roger;
with my love and thanks.

INTRODUCTION

THIS BOOK WAS WRITTEN in the belief that the role of cycling in the social history of the Western World has been sadly underestimated. Some social historians fail to mention cycling even when it was the principal recreation or form of transport of those they are describing. There are also histories of transport which seem to denigrate anything without an engine. Cycling was, especially from the late nineteenth century onwards, an important and exciting agent of social change. It became a battleground for all manner of Victorian values: propriety versus public pleasure, aged wisdom versus youthful indiscipline, femininity versus emancipation, the exclusivity of amateur gentlemen in sport versus the brashness of working-class professionals. The basic but incomparably efficient act of propelling oneself on an arrangement of wheels is still able to upset established values, as cycling has revived in the midst of the motor age.

The history of cycling is rich and varied. Ideas, attitudes and excitement have flowed from exceptional individuals to social groups, from class to class and from nation to nation. This book is therefore unavoidably broad in its scope and international in content. It includes the vogue for 'running-machines' in Germany, the efforts of amateur inventors in Europe and America, and the boneshaker craze which began in France. The ensuing cult of the almost paramilitary clubmen was international in extent, and the great cycling boom of the 1890s included the Society ladies of London, the new millionaires of the United States, the bush-cyclists of Australia and the middle classes of all industrialised countries. Cycling went on to become an important element in the daily lives, and sometimes the politics, of millions of working-class Europeans before it was pushed aside by the advent of motoring. Just when cycling was in danger of becoming a sub-cultural activity in the West, it became a generally liberating and harmonious form of transport in countries such as China.

I have tried to integrate all modes of cycling, from delivery boys on carrier tricycles to élite athletes riding technology derived from space programmes. I have found great pleasure in the variety of cycling's history, but have left much untouched. There is enormous scope for further research and study.

Wherever possible, I refer to cycle-types by the names given them during the period of their use but I have occasionally departed from this practice in the interests of clarity.

1
THE PREHISTORY OF CYCLING

Ancestral Vehicles

IN 1966 THE MONKS of Grottoferrata near Rome made a remarkable discovery during their restoration of Leonardo da Vinci's manuscripts on behalf of the Italian government. In detaching a sheet from its backing paper they uncovered a rough sketch of a bicycle which was very similar in its basic features to machines which did not become standard till four centuries later. They found the sketch alongside some pornographic drawings and a caricature of one of da Vinci's pupils. All the drawings seem to have originated from his studio in the 1490s, and seem to have been the work of his unruly pupils. The bicycle sketch is certainly not by da Vinci, but may have been a copy of one of his drawings or models. It astonished the experts and there

1 The bicycle drawing discovered among Leonardo da Vinci's manuscripts, but probably the work of a pupil.

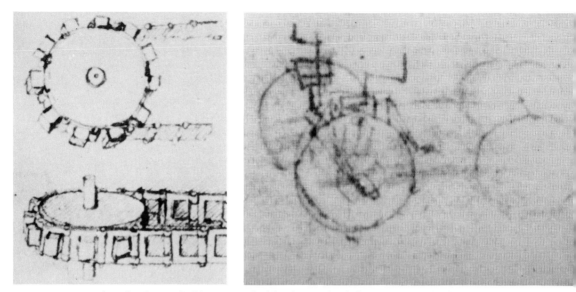

2 A sketch of a probably unworkable chainwheel design uniquely found in Leonardo's notebooks, and similar to the chainwheel in the bicycle drawing. He elsewhere drew transmission chains almost identical to the modern bicycle chain.

3 Leonardo da Vinci's design for a hand-cranked carriage.

were spontaneous but unspecific challenges to its authenticity. However, the vigorous scepticism of critics has failed to undermine any of the evidence for authenticity set out by Professor Augusto Marinoni, the leading da Vinci scholar. The vehicle drawn may well have been no more than an inspired flight of fancy, especially since, with no apparent means of steering, it would have been unrideable. Such elementary design omissions were common in da Vinci's 'invention drawings'. Whatever the machine's significance his notebooks show that the technology needed for a sophisticated bicycle was at hand. They contain drawings and descriptions of ball-bearings, gearing systems, continuous drive-chains, freewheels and band-brakes: much of which would have been familiar, if in more basic forms, to other Renaissance technologists and to military engineers in particular. Apart from the chain transmission system none of these design concepts can be associated with the bicycle drawing; they serve simply as a reminder that, in the matter of cycle design, technology often preceded imaginative insight and practical application.[1]

The small number of human-powered vehicles actually built before the nineteenth century were of little use as practical transport. They were mostly variations of the horseless carriage: eye-catching rarities built for amusement and propelled at great effort, often by servant labour. Among the earliest were the purpose-built theme floats used in the carnival parades of the mediaeval Italian city states. These decorated carriages had human engines ingeniously concealed within them. In the late fifteenth century Leonardo da Vinci was occasionally employed on their design and his notebooks include a sketch of a four-wheeled chassis which may have been intended for carnival purposes. Each front wheel in this early quadricycle drawing is driven by a separate hand-crank.

In Northern Europe the few known human-powered processional carriages were massively and pompously decorated, far removed from the simple frivolity of earlier Italian versions, and were used on more ceremonial or triumphal occasions. In 1649 the *Nuremberg Chronicle* reported that a compass-maker of that city, Johann Hautsch, had made an ornamental carriage which 'goes at 2000 paces an hour and can stop when you want it to and go again when you want it to, and, indeed, this is all done by clockwork'. The vehicle was bought by the Crown Prince of Sweden and became a big attraction on his coronation parade. Another Hautsch carriage, built for the King of Denmark, was hand-cranked by children hidden inside.[2] Such inefficient status-enhancing vehicles were playthings of the powerful, ancestors not of the bicycle but of the motor car.

Around 1680, some thirty years after Hautsch's first machine, a totally different kind of horseless carriage was built in a village outside Nuremberg. Stephan Farffler, a paraplegic clockmaker (some sources say bell-maker) made himself a hand-cranked tricycle, and later a quadricycle. Another

4 In the 1680s Stephan Farffler of Altdorf, near Nuremberg, drove himself to church each Sunday on an invalid tricycle of his own making.

5 A treadle-driven carriage built by Jackman of London in about 1760; here being driven in the grounds of the Nymphenburg Palace, Munich.

self-propelled invalid carriage, the *fauteuil à roulette* (chair on wheels), was developed in France in the mid-eighteenth century. In 1758 it was described in the advertising journal *Annonces-Affiches* as being 'a handsome chair mounted on three wheels with spring suspension, suitable for an invalid who, by means of hand-levers, may progress around his chamber or garden'.

Most other references to human-powered vehicles between about 1650 and 1800 reveal a certain unity of design. They were typically built in the manner of horse carriages but with a luckless footman employed in bouncing on treadles or on a cranked rear axle, while his master sat in front steering with reins. Such machines were seen around Padua, Genoa, Bologna, Munich and Paris in the late 1600s, and in Paris and London in the 1700s. Some were used on city streets—Dr Elie Richard's vehicle was laboured around Paris for several years in the 1690s—but most were confined to the smoother drives of parks and country estates. These gentlemen's pleasure carriages were intended for private amusement. However, from about 1800 to 1860 inventors joined a more earnest quest for a hand-propelled (manumotive) or foot-propelled (pedomotive) carriage which would be both successful and popular. There was a tendency towards complexity, a feature perhaps derived from the spellbinding heavyweight steam technology of the age. Most advances were confined to Britain and France where innovation was helped along by better technology and roads, and by the more organised communication of ideas.

The Running-Machine

In 1817 the path of complex experimentation was sidestepped by a simple invention from the remote forests of Central Germany, a country then not yet industrialised. From this socially and technologically underdeveloped area came a device which was to catch the fancy of the fashionable world. It consisted of a wooden body above two wooden wheels set in line. The rider scooted along by pushing his feet alternately against the ground whilst steering the front wheel. The inventor of this running-machine (*Laufmaschine*) was Baron Karl von Drais, Master of the Forests in the Dutchy of Baden. He had first 'invented' a four-wheeled pedomotive carriage and had unsuccessfully hawked it around the aristocracy of Europe, to which his own noble birth gave him some access. He became disenchanted with mechanical propulsion, a reaction which partly explains the functional simplicity of his running-machine. However, opting out of the design consensus also involved a leap of the imagination: it was by no means obvious that a single-track vehicle could travel without tipping over. With the exception of the footwork, the art of balancing on Drais's invention was

6 The running-machine of Baron von Drais.

little different from that of cycling today in that it was based on a subtle series of compensatory steering adjustments and body movements. Two wheels also made for a lighter, more efficient and more manoeuvrable machine, allowing the rider to take the firmest part of the roadway, or better still the pedestrian walkway. Drais began limited manufacture and hoped to make good business. His machines were fitted with an upholstered seat, a luggage rack and a 'balancing board' against which the rider pressed his elbows to assist the machine along. There was also a cord-operated brake and a prop-stand, and the seat height could be adjusted. At least one machine was fitted with a milometer, in about 1825. What would have been the most useful accessory, a pair of drive-cranks, was assiduously avoided. Drais also offered three- and four-wheeled versions so that one or more men might take ladies for a jaunt. He launched into a long marketing and patenting campaign, part of which involved sending advertising letters to leading figures, including several kings. On good roads his 'running-machine' could beat the horse and was probably the fastest road vehicle in existence. In time trials it proved itself four times faster than local post coaches.

Those who bought Drais's machine suffered considerably more than coach travellers in that they had a more intimate relationship with the road. The roads of Europe had been deteriorating since Roman times and most were churned up by carriage and ox-cart traffic. Drais's running-machines jolted over the solid ruts and sank deep into the soft ones. It was difficult to keep up momentum and hill-climbing was rarely possible. The lack of suspension punished the rider's body, while the constant pounding against uneven road surfaces could bring foot injuries and pulled muscles. In wet weather the machine slithered about; feet failed to grip and were constantly soaked in puddles. On many occasions it would have been faster and more comfortable to walk.

Despite all discomforts Drais, and thousands after him, found the running-machine worthwhile. The Baron rode his machine around his locality and on forestry inspection tours. However, local opinion had no time for such eccentricity and he was often abused. There was even a children's chant:

Freiherr von Rutsch,
Zum Fahren kein Kutsch,
Zum Reiten kein Gaul,
Zum Laufen zu faul!

The Baron Slip-Slide,
No carriage to ride,
Won't sit on a nag,
Finds walking a fag!

7 An 1817 German drawing of riders on a rutted track. Their machines, made by Schwalbach of Dresden, have seat springs, leg protection, prop-stands and lanterns.

On the 12 January 1818 Drais patented his machine in Baden and on the 17 February he had a French patent taken out, hoping for a warm welcome in Paris. On the 25 March the *Petite Chronique de Paris* proclaimed:

> Long live this worthy Baron von Drais to whom we shall owe such novel pleasures! We have named his horseless vehicles *Draisiennes* ... What pleasant exercise this carriage will provide! It will cover two, three or even four leagues in an hour, depending on the terrain! Our wellbeing will increase no less than our pleasure, and I do not doubt that there will be doctors to prescribe these terrestrial carriages just as they used to prescribe the overhead carriages [*chars aériens*—presumably a kind of cable car] ... Be quick to sharpen your pens, you chroniclers of fashion! Very soon the races will commence. It will be a second Longchamp, and imagine how our womenfolk will be infatuated with the velocipede when they learn how effortlessly a gallant can drive a lady along, as is done on sleigh-rides.

All did not go well for Drais in Paris. He failed to attend the first major public demonstration of his Draisienne (as it became generally called) in the Luxembourg Gardens on the 5 April 1818. He was in Frankfurt at the time, giving a lecture on his invention to the Society for the Advancement of the Practical Arts, and so sent in his stead one of his forest huntsmen. This man, who was unused to his master's machine, was to perform together with a Monsieur Garçin, the holder of the Draisienne sales franchise in Paris. The huntsman, being particularly slow, failed to shake off a crowd of mocking children and got off to push at least once. The occasion was only enlivened when a bystander, who thought he could do better, leapt on a Draisienne and tumbled off spectacularly. When a crucial nut was lost the demonstration was abandoned.[3]

Some lost prestige was restored by a few organised races and further exhibitions at the Luxembourg and Tivoli Gardens, and Paris began to warm to the Draisienne. It was honoured and splendidly advertised by a play, *Les Vélocipèdes*, which opened at the Théâtre des Variétés on the 13 May 1818. There was much Draisienne hiring at the fairs around the outskirts of the city, and also in the summer gardens, where lady-carrying versions were particularly popular. It seems that Draisiennes were closely associated with places of entertainment such as fairgrounds, amusement parks and theatres; and they were ridden in a corresponding spirit of fun. That few riders took them as seriously as the inventor himself may have averted much public derision. On the 20 July 1818 the *Petite Chronique de Paris* reported that 'we have not noticed any tendency to ridicule those who try out these new machines'. There is little evidence that the aristocracy of Paris ever took more than a conversational interest in the phenomenon.

8 The antics of velocipeding gentlemen astonish the hard-working country people of the vineyards around Mannheim.

Having registered as many patents as he could, and launched his invention in Paris, Drais left his forestry post to devote himself to his running-machine business. He hoped to set up a manufactory before long. Yet his machine was so basic in its form and function that it was copied on a large scale. Drais had not been able to register patents in all of the many independent German states, and even the patents he held were generally disregarded. Mainly as a result of Paris publicity news of the invention was broadcast by the press to the European metropolises. Soon illegal versions of his machine were being made in various parts of France, and a carriage-works in Vienna provided machines for an associated 'running machine riding school' set up in early 1818 opposite the Imperial Military Academy. There were also four independent makers of running-machines in Dresden, the most prominent being the carriage-maker Schwalbach.[4] The vogue was extensive, whatever the legality of the machines ridden. In 1818 J. W. Goethe observed the students of Jena riding on running-machines on the Paradies, an open-air gymnastics ground. They were ridden in the Netherlands, where the Mayor of Haarlem owned one, and in Milan, where they made such an impact that they were banned by civic order in September that year.

According to one unsupported source[5] Drais travelled to London around 1818 and had a running-machine constructed by a mechanic named Knight. However, the major craze which affected England in the early part of 1819 was kindled by a machine based on the Drais principle but otherwise designed by Denis Johnson of London. Johnson showed all the entrepreneurial skills found lacking in Drais. As a carriage maker he had a professional understanding of design, manufacturing and marketing techniques. He applied for a patent on the 22 December 1818, making no reference to Drais, although he knew of the Drais original.

Johnson's machines had wooden, and later iron, bodies which dipped in the middle to allow for bigger wheels and a correspondingly better ride. The wheels were of wood, strengthened by hoops of iron: narrow rims for indoor use, wide rims for road machines. Handlebar, chest-rest and wheel-forks were all of slender iron. Johnson christened it the 'Pedestrian Curricle' but the nicknames 'dandy-horse' and 'hobby-horse' caught on and stuck. The hobby-horse was altogether a more refined beast than the Draisienne (or 'Draisine' as Drais himself had come to call it by this time). Johnson's machine was manufactured in quantity, using techniques beyond the reach of amateur constructors. Apart from an early modification to the steering

9 A Viennese riding school which operated in early 1818 opposite the Imperial Military Academy.

19

10 Johnson's Pedestrian Hobby Horse Riding School, London, where leisured gentlemen learned to ride in 1819. The artist was Henry Alken.

11 An exaggerated depiction of the English hobby-horse craze of 1819.

mechanism his design remained virtually unchanged till hobbies ceased to be used. The Draisienne, on the other hand, was a cumbersome product of a wood-dependent technology, and was easily copied by amateurs or by carriage-makers on a 'one-off' basis. As a result there was huge variety in design throughout Europe.

Johnson opened riding schools in Brewer Street and the Strand, where he personally instructed fashionable purchasers and where machines were hired out. His demonstration rides were far removed from the Draisienne fiasco in the Luxembourg Gardens. The *Liverpool Mercury* commented:

> Before we saw the performance of Mr Johnson, who exhibits at the Music-Hall . . . we had no conception of the graceful movements of which [this machine] is capable in skilful hands. Skaiting [sic] has always been considered as the most elegant recreation; but velocipeding (or whatever it may be called) is, in our opinion, more pleasing, as performed by the gentleman we have mentioned.[6]

Johnson was more fortunate than Drais in that he had on his doorstep a leisured, novelty-seeking clientele: the sporty bucks of Regency London. Good business was made as notable figures took to scooting around the streets and parks. Bets were taken on hobbies beating stage coaches, and one practitioner beat a four-horse coach to Brighton by half an hour. A shoemaker found it worthwhile to sell velocipeding boots with iron plates on the soles; but few can have made more capital out of the craze than the caricaturists and their print shops. Many of them used the hobby to ridicule leading social or political figures. In one caricature, the wayward Prince Regent is seen stretched out—although still noticeably obese—on an elongated hobby-horse, at the same time making a comfortable seat for his portly mistress. In another the reputedly spendthrift Duke of York rides a hobby-horse as John Bull exclaims: 'Dang it, . . . thee art saving indeed; thee used to ride in a coach and six, and now I pay thee £10,000 a year more thee art riding a wooden horse, for all the world like a gate-post!'
One satirist wrote of

> Patent pedestrian accellerators,
> Floating velocipedes, perambulators,
> Or hobbies, at present which so much the rage are,
> That asses from Brighton they'll banish, I wager.[7]

12 The Duke of York.

The obsessions of the caricaturists and satirists give us no firm idea as to the extent of the craze. But one clue is provided by John Badcock in his *Slang Dictionary* of 1823. After defining 'dandy-horse' he adds that at the height of the craze 'hundreds of such might be seen in a day'. Another clue lies in the fact that the authorities found it necessary to ban hobby riders from the foot pavements, and then to suppress the activity more generally. In March 1819 a London press dispatch used in American newspapers reported that 'the crowded state of the metropolis does not admit of this novel mode of exercise, and it has been put down by the Magistrate of Police'.[8] It does not seem, however, that road riding was ever made illegal in London.

There was some hobby riding outside the capital. In 1819 M. W. Field of Birmingham was advertising and exhibiting his velocipedes (presumably made under licence from Johnson). We know that at least six hobby riders travelled the three miles between Ipswich and Whitton in fifteen minutes every evening, and in County Durham one of a group of riders careering down a hill ran down a young boy, broke his leg and failed to stop.[9] Riders venturing into unenlightened rural areas could expect trouble. One gentleman on the road to Camberwell 'attracted a great crowd, from the pressure of which he was, at his earnest solicitation, extracted by a passing coachman, who carried him and his horse off on the roof'.[10] By July 1819 the craze was tailing off. Legal restrictions had blunted the fun, doctors had warned of 'ruptures and inflamations of certain muscles of the thighs and legs', and caricaturists had savaged the self-regarding.

There was a short-lived craze on the Eastern Seaboard of the United States in mid-1819, as the British craze was losing wind. Its origins are not clear. Hobbies (known simply as 'velocipedes' in the USA) were being made in Boston in April 1819, where the students of Harvard took pleasure in wheeling over the old bridge on moonlit nights. Two months later machines based on the Johnson design appeared in Troy, 120 miles inland, and were hired out to young men about town for twenty-five cents an hour. Davis and Rogers, the local machinists who made these vehicles, were the first to introduce velocipedes to New York. We also know that Denis Johnson arrived in New York in 1819 to promote his hobby-horses just as they were first appearing in the city. It is possible that the Troy machinists were his local agents. Although riding schools suddenly appeared in the larger Eastern cities interest was most intense in New York, where the timid rode at nightfall along the Bowery, and the adventurous took pleasure in rolling down a long hill to City Hall Park. Wheel-less devotees watched velocipeding exhibitions at a rink set up near Bowling Green. At the midsummer height of the craze an enormous crowd of New Yorkers waited for hours in the rain for an advertised demonstration of a velocipede's speed. No ride took place, it having been a hoax. The American press was no less mocking than the caricaturists of London. The *Federal Republican and Baltimore*

13 A Cruikshank caricature of June 1819. The sign above the door reads: 'A fine stud of REAL HORSES to be sold as cheap as dogs' meat—the present proprietor going into the Hobby Line.'

Telegraph informed its readers that 'A curious two-wheeled vehicle called the Velocipede has been invented, which is propelled by *Jack-asses* instead of horses' (9 July 1819). The roads were worse than in Britain and sidewalk riding was common; so much so that velocipeding was prohibited in New York City.

The American craze had been a final spasm. Ridicule, legal restrictions, bad roads and change of fashion had all contributed to the demise. In addition, the strains and injuries suffered by riders may have been a greatly under-rated problem, being too intimate and prosaic to merit press attention. Many unwanted machines were handed on to youths. There are various accounts of fifteen to seventeen year olds draisienne-touring around France in the 1820s, and one as late as 1848. The German homeland of the draisienne had missed the full force of the international craze, and caught up a little in the 1820s. The earliest known draisienne race in Germany was in 1829 when twenty-six riders competed for prize money in Munich. A newspaper report on this race mentions that the Munich cartwright Semmler, maker of the winning machine, was selling wooden ones at twenty-five gulden and iron ones at fifty-five gulden, and that he hired machines out. German royalty also took a late interest in the draisienne. Some time after Prince Alexander, brother of Kaiser Wilhelm III, ordered a machine from Drais.

Drais persisted in advocating his machines, and in 1832 he was promoting an 'improved' version in England of all places. Disappointment had soured his innocent, open nature, and he had turned to alcohol. He was stripped of his title of Chamberlain, following a brawl in a tavern, and strongly suspected of insanity. In the hope of financial salvation he continued to produce inventions, including, in 1842, the earliest known human-powered rail-car. It was, according to Drais, faster than the Mannheim to Heidelberg locomotive, could transport passengers who had missed the train, and provided a hygienic and personally controllable form of transport. The arrival of the railways provided a welcome alternative to the dire roads which, among other things, had so restricted the popularity of Drais's running-machine. Financial success again escaped him and he spent his latter years as a travelling showman. He died impoverished in 1851, aged sixty-six.

Amateur Mechanics

The Industrial Revolution did not clasp the velocipede to its mechanical heart. Coal and Capital were intent on using the power of steam to break through the traditional limitations of Nature. In an age much taken with large-scale alternatives to animal and human-power there was little interest among professional engineers in the development of human-powered vehicles. The leading transport engineers were folk heroes whose brave deeds were measured in fast trains, daring bridges and tunnels, and prestigious passenger liners. Yet such was the public fascination in Britain for the application of technology that a growing number of amateur mechanics joined the welter of invention. Some were 'self-improving' factory workers and artisans. They were likely to be among the 120,000 members of the 700 or so mechanics' institutes active up and down the country by the year 1841. Many men, self-taught in this way, were to become leading professional engineers. There were also amateurs of middle-class background, often subscribing to local scientific libraries. It was the enthusiasts of the back yard and tool shed who experimented in velocipede design while the engineers and factories busied themselves with other things. The amateurs' experimenting, which was particularly energetic in the 1820s, was based on three or four-wheeled vehicles, but almost every other design question remained open for debate, and little agreement could be found. Was arm-power more efficient than leg-power? Was rotary action better than treadle-drive? Or should one pull on levers much as one rows a boat? Should steering be at the front or the back, direct or indirect? The velocipede inventors recognised the importance of their pioneering work. They were looking for that elusive combination of mechanical principles which would (and eventually did) being efficient personal mobility to the population at large. Their miscellaneous designs were imaginative, impressive and some-times bizarre; but their preference for complicated tricycles and quadri-cycles blocked any useful development. Such machines made for heavy work on the flat, and became dangerously difficult to steer and brake going downhill.

14 Bramley and Parker's machine of 1830 was a tandem tricycle—the nearside wheel is omitted in the drawing. It combined hand-cranking and treadle-drive.

The amateur mechanics were helped towards a communal sense of pur-pose by the *Mechanics' Magazine*, founded in 1823, and joined by the *English Mechanic* in 1869. They acted as information exchanges. Readers sent in descriptions of their inventions and were given a platform for their experiences and views. Along with velocipede discussions were items on such matters as aquatic perambulators, mechanical boatswains, har-moniums, steam ploughs, improved window blinds, the Indian method of cutting precious stones, and air-tight night soil carts. The magazines were democratic in their outlook (if the absence of contributions from women allows such a description), and the standard form of address was 'brother mechanic'. Among velocipede designers mentioned in the *Mechanics'*

25

Magazine were a blacksmith, a surgeon, a teacher, a wheelwright, a surveyor and a shoemaker.

The *Mechanics' Magazine*'s editorial had less than full confidence in the potential of the velocipede. On the 21 April 1832 readers were told that 'Man is a locomotive machine of Nature's own making, and not to be improved on by the addition of any cranks or wheels of mortal invention'. On the 5 May came a spirited reply from a reader:

> Now, Sir, I once skated a mile in four minutes, which is a rate of velocity far exceeding anything ever accomplished by the naked foot; and on untying my velocipedes I found they were made not by Dame Nature but by Giles Handsaw of Ironmonger Lane, London. What saith thy philosophy to this, good Mr Editor?

There were also reflections on social aspects of velocipeding, such as this stupefying example of Victorian phraseology: 'It is true, that with men of expensive habits, whose self-satisfaction would be reduced in proportion to their diminution of external show, an engine so economical and unobtrusive [as a velocipede] would find but little patronage' (*Mechanics' Magazine*, 28 November 1829). Sometimes homely advice was imparted: 'The man who makes a daily trial of his present skill is sure to go ahead, whether his hobby is towards the harmonium, organ, fly-fishing, velocipedism, or the less dignified progress on stilts' (*English Mechanic*, 16 July 1869). Occasionally such earnest sentiments were offset by items of amusing naïveté. Alongside the above letter was the following submission, which shows a mistrust of the pedallable two-wheeled machines just at the moment when they finally established themselves:

Sir, I propose a hot air balloon velocipede. My object is to secure the perpendicularity of the machine by a balloon just large enough for that purpose, thereby securing confidence in the rider, at the same time it will assist the machine in climbing hills and passing over rough roads. There is an oil lamp to supply the balloon with hot air. The opinion of some brother correspondents on the merits of the balloon will interest me.

W. T. Trindon.

On the whole amateur mechanics built machines for their own pleasure and personal use. However a few professional craftsmen were able to produce commercially successful quadricycles. The most prominent was Willard Sawyer, a carpenter in Dover who, between about 1845 and 1868, manufactured and marketed quadricycles of highly refined craftsmanship. They had wooden frames, slender wooden wheels, and treadle-drive directly attached to a cranked wrought-iron axle. The range of designs included a scaled-down *Youth's Carriage* and an *Invalid's Carriage*. There was also the *Tourist and Traveller* which, according to the catalogue, was 'designed for persons of itinerant habits or avocations having more taste for freedom than ceremony'. There was the *Promenade and Visiting Carriage* which was 'suitable for Military Officers wishing to unite the pleasure of sightseeing with the profit of exercise'. Sawyer also recommended this machine for ministers of the Church with remote flocks, and for lawyers who visited clients. There was also a *Lady's Carriage* with dress guards, a *Racer* which weighed only sixty-three pounds, and a *Sociable* which could carry any number up to six. Sawyer's products were aimed at as wide a market as

15 Willard Sawyer on one of his velocipedes.

possible. They were graded according to quality (first, second and third class), and differed greatly in price: his third class youth's machine cost from £3 to £4, whereas the *Park Sociable*, which he developed later in his career, cost fifty guineas. He was able to attract aristocratic and royal patronage. The Prince of Wales, having visited Sawyer's workshop in Dover, was presented with a velocipede, and subsequently the Emperor of Russia ordered one. Sawyer's business seems to have faded away as two-wheeled boneshakers became popular in the late 1860s.

In the United States multi-wheeled velocipede experimentation was unremarkable until it blossomed with breath-taking variety around 1869, having been stimulated by the fashion for boneshakers in that year (to be described later). The American inventors were less conservative in their designs and more commercial in their outlook than their British counterparts. Many of the 183 velocipede patents of 1869 were handled by the *Scientific American* Patent Agency. The magazine published illustrations and detailed descriptions, and invited manufacturers to get in touch with the inventors.

A major American design theme was the monocycle: a single large wheel propelled by a rider sitting inside it. One version was the Wheelosipede, invented by a resident of Troy. It was paddled along like a hobby-horse and recommended for the transportation of sand and other building materials. According to the *Troy Times* it was set to supersede 'all the bicycles and descriptions of velocipedes'. A ten-foot monocycle in Pittsburg was reported as covering a mile in two minutes when propelled by a team of five men occupying 'seats on the automatic horse ... as comfortable as in a carriage'. History has left us no record of how they were fitted inside the wheel, nor of how they stayed there. Monocycles were heavy and unwieldy, and dangerous when revolving downhill. Some designs required the rider to be caged in by the addition of metal side-pieces before the wheel was set rolling. This prevented him from falling free in emergencies. Also in 1869, a Cincinnati gentleman was constructing a clockwork velocipede which was, he fondly asserted, to be kept in continuous motion by the rider winding it up each time it was about to run down. There were several patents for adaptations to allow bicycles to travel on railway lines. One inventor claimed a speed of 60 m.p.h., another hoped for 100 m.p.h. and a test run by a third inventor produced 20 m.p.h. over fifty-five miles. There was a separate adaptation for riding on horse-car (omnibus) tracks.[11] Velocipede patents continued to be registered long after the 1869 bonanza. The *Scientific American* of 2 May 1887 detailed a monstrous Swing Bicycle reportedly built by Nathaniel Brown of Emporia, Kansas. By pulling down on handles the riders made the suspended basket in which they sat swing like a pendulum, the effect of which was to propel the machine along.

Amusingly unrealistic velocipede designs can be found in the patent

16 The Swing Bicycle of Nathaniel Brown, Kansas. By pulling down on levers the basket was made to swing like a pendulum, which induced the machine to roll along. Steering was effected by one rider pulling harder than the other.

records of many countries, and at relatively late dates in areas away from the mainstream. In 1878 C. A. Haab of Switzerland patented a pneumatic-powered carriage which involved the operator squeezing bellows with his feet. In the same year Max Felix Schmidt of Görlitz, Bavaria, patented a 'riding car' which required the operator to bounce up and down on a seat. His energies were allegedly transmitted to the rear axle by a series of cogs.[12] At least three American and one German patent involved rocking-horses attached by cranks to wheels.

No inventor's efforts, whether practical or crackpot, can be seen in isolation from the unhelpful state of the road surfaces. For example, the big wheels of the monocycles and the Swing Bicycle were intended to over-ride unevennesses. A radical response was to avoid the roads entirely, as happened with the rail-adapted machines, and an American inventor devised a velocipede with caterpillar tracks.

Macmillan and Lefèbvre: Progress without Progeny

It is difficult to understand why the idea of adding mechanically transmitted leg-power to a two-wheeled vehicle (to produce a bicycle) did not make its great public appearance until the 1860s. Drais had already shown, in 1817, the overriding advantages of two wheels and that one could stay upright on them; and the amateur mechanics had spent the following half century developing all manner of transmission systems. In fact, the two elements were put together on several occasions before the 1860s, but failed to catch the world's attention. There were isolated examples of draisienne-type machines fitted with front wheel drive; but of more interest are two remarkably visionary vehicles which seem to have been in use in the early 1840s, each with two wheels and rear-wheel-drive.

The first was made in about 1839 by Kirkpatrick Macmillan, a blacksmith-mechanic from a village near Dumfries, Scotland. He was an unambitious man, being content to ride his machine locally and let it be copied here and there by other local mechanics. There is no record of his trying to publicise his invention in national magazines, nor of any attempts at marketing. And yet his machine was a gazelle compared to the elephantine quadricycles of the period. It was fleet enough to take him on a 140 mile

17 McCall's bicycle, built in the 1860s and thought to be similar to a previous machine built by Kirkpatrick Macmillan in 1839. The treadle design is like the power transmission on locomotives of the period, which had a piston-driven crank attached to an eccentric point on the drive-wheel.

round trip to Glasgow in 1842. The following report of the outcome of that trip, which appeared in the *Glasgow Argus* of the 9 June, has not been verified by any other source and must be treated with appropriate caution:

> On Wednesday a gentleman, who stated he came from Thornhill in Dumfries, was placed at the Gorbals public bar, charged with riding along the pavement on a velocipede to the obstruction of the passage, and with having, by so doing, thrown over a child. It appeared from his statement that he had on the day previous come all the way from Old Cumnock, a distance of 40 miles, bestriding the velocipede, and that he performed the journey in the space of five hours. On reaching the Barony of Gorbals he had gone upon the pavement, and was surrounded by a large crowd, attracted by the novelty of the machine. The child who was thrown down had not sustained any injury, and under the circumstances the offender was fined only 5 shillings. The velocipede employed in this instance was very ingeniously constructed—it moved on wheels, turned with the hand by means of a crank; but to make it 'progress' appeared to require more labour than will be compensated for by the increase of speed. This invention will not supersede the railway.

The reference to hand-cranking is probably a reporter's error but cannot be ignored as Macmillan's original machine has not survived. However, a surviving copy constructed just four years after the Glasgow ride, by the cooper Dalzell, incorporated the all-important foot-treadles to the rear wheel, and without Dalzell claiming any major design innovation. Another factor in favour of foot-treadles is the newspaper report that Macmillan rode forty miles at 8 m.p.h. Twenty-five years later riders of much lighter, finer velocipedes would be hard put to match this speed on the smooth asphalt of Paris. A hand-cranked machine would have made Macmillan's achievement most unlikely. A number of copies of his machine were built commercially in the 1860s by Thomas McCall, a joiner and wheelwright in Kilmarnock, and were ridden by McCall in Glasgow race events in which he beat the by then standard front-wheel-drive bicycles.

The other precocious machine appears to have been made and ridden in about 1842 by Alexandre Lefèbvre of St Denis, near Paris. His machine was similar in design to the Macmillan copies, but more refined. In 1860 or 1861 Lefèbvre emigrated to California, taking his velocipede with him. Here he continued to make velocipedes (of an undetermined kind) without ever achieving fame. His original machine has survived and is held to be the world's oldest existing bicycle.[13]

Both Macmillan and Lefèbvre were men of talent and inspiration, but were too isolated, geographically and otherwise, to have a major influence on velocipede development.

2
THE BONESHAKER MANIA

The Craze in France

AFTER CENTURIES OF FALSE STARTS and futile hopes, cycling (or 'velociped-ing' as it was then called) finally established itself in the 1860s in Paris. Two-wheeled velocipedes, characterised by pedals and cranks on the front wheel, had at last been introduced to a receptive market and interest quick-ened to a collective passion around 1868 and 1869. In Britain they were nicknamed 'boneshakers', but in this chapter the generic and international term 'velocipede' will be used. They were a gift for Parisian Affairs corres-pondents, who dispatched some vivid reportage: 'Paris is just now afflicted with a serious nuisance . . . velocipedes, machines like the ghosts of departed spiders, on which horrible boys and detestable men career about the streets and boulevards' (*Once a Week*, 21 March 1868). The new velocipedes, described by these observers as ghostly spiders and predatory dragonflies, evoked wonder and delight in others. The boulevards were similarly busy ten months later. In the May 1869 issue of *Girl of the Period Miscellany* it was reported that

> Velocipedes have become quite a social institution in Paris, and velo-cipeding as necessary an accomplishment as dancing or riding. The veloceman, as he styles himself, is to be seen in all his glory careering at full speed through the shady avenues of the Bois de Boulogne, or skim-ming like some giant dragonfly over the level surface of the roads inter-secting the Champs-Elysées. The converging avenues of the Arc de l'Etoile are amongst his favourite hunting grounds; there he disports himself continually, to the terror of the aged and the short-winded.

'Oh, Velocipede! Camel of the Occident!' wrote another enthusiastic jour-nalist.

For the first time large numbers of people could enjoy fast personal transport without the expense of keeping or hiring a carriage. Riders in Paris

18 A recurring theme in nineteenth-century photography: sensationalism mas-querading as emancipation. It is, however, likely that the lady in this Viennese studio shot rode her velocipede for a living.

could appreciate the qualities and potential of their new vehicles in a variety of ways, not all of them limited to the asphalted avenues of Napoleon III's grandiosely reconstructed city centre. There were, for example, at least two spacious and elegant indoor riding schools where many of those who had mastered the basic art of self-propulsion graduated to velocipede gymnastics, now disparagingly called 'trick riding'. Also, velocipedes were available in most of the privately owned gymnasia. Skilful 'velocipedestrians' entertained the crowds by riding hands-off along the narrow stone parapets of the Seine, and by performing breath-taking gymnastic feats while riding down the 101 steps of the Trocadero Palace (since demolished). To the west of the city youths raced informally along the leafy lanes of the Bois de Boulogne, and 'velocipede boats' were for hire on the lakes of the wood. At the Parc de Saint-Cloud, on the southern edge of the Bois, a wide cross-section of Parisian society turned out regularly to watch gaudily dressed competitors rattle their machines around a race track. Many civil servants able to afford a machine rode to their offices from the suburbs, and velocipeding messenger boys were employed by newspapers and by the Bourse stock exchange. At night in Paris velocipedes with lanterns swinging in front of them darted among the carriages like fire-flies (velocipeding lends itself so easily to creature similes). Some riders strapped miniature lanterns to their chests; and velocipedes displaying illuminated advertisements were sent out by enterprising tradesmen. Velocipedes also found their way into the theatres and music halls, where scantily dressed women rode acrobatically.[1]

The initiator of the whole social phenomenon was Pierre Michaux, variously described as a cabinet-maker, locksmith and carriage repairer. With the help of his son, Ernest, he conceived and constructed the first machines in workshops by the Champs Elysées in 1861. Apart from the cranks and pedals early versions showed a draisienne lineage, and their wooden bodies and wheels gave a dull, jarring ride. Although putting feet on pedals was a huge advance in design it also led to steering problems, as it was difficult to steer and pedal the same wheel simultaneously. When the wheel rim made contact with the rider's inside leg it caused trouser-wear and chafing, and also deposited on him various kinds of débris from the road. A velocipede-riding manual advised that 'our pupil may fairly add the value of six pairs of trousers to his outlay'.[2] Some riders took to wearing high leather boots. The early Michaulines (as the Michaux machines came to be called) failed to improve on the draisienne's road-holding characteristics. They slipped and skidded on muddy earth roads, as well as on wet paved ones. The introduction of solid rubber tyres in the late 1860s improved comfort and handling.

In 1865 Michaux et Compagnie made about 400 machines: just over one a day. Then, in 1866–67, they developed and introduced a new model. It had an elegant wrought-iron body which tapered down at the back to hold

19 French racing velocipedists on Michaulines, about 1868. Pedalling with the arch of the foot was the standard practice.

the rear wheel. The front wheel had been made larger to carry the rider further with each revolution of the pedals, and various other refinements had been added. Michaux publicised the new model at the World Exhibition of 1867 in Paris, and he booked an encouraging number of orders.[3] He also received an order from the head of state, Napoleon III, who was an invalid. Once the royal velocipede had been delivered, Michaux (always aware of the value of royal patronage) supplied the Prince Imperial, Louis-Napoleon, with a *vélocipède de luxe* of rosewood and aluminium-bronze. The prince, in turn, presented twelve child-size velocipedes to aristocratic playmates, and such was his enthusiasm that an opposition faction called him 'Vélocipède IV'. His rides along the streets of Paris and in the Tuileries Gardens were a priceless public advertisement for Michaux and encouraged velocipeding among the socially high-placed. The wealthy and titled frequented the riding schools or practised in the seclusion of private courtyards. House-party guests at country chateaux arranged velocipede races among themselves, and when the rich of Paris holidayed at the coast they took to velocipeding along the sea-front promenades.

As the vogue developed the Michaux works proved to be severely under-capitalised and faced competition from other makers. However, an invest-ment of 100,000 francs from the Olivier Brothers financed a move to a new 2½ acre (10,000 m²) factory near the Arc de Triomphe. The Olivier Brothers gradually took over the concern and it was renamed the 'Compagnie Parisienne des Vélocipèdes'. In late 1869, or early 1870, Michaux was happy

35

20 Top-of-the-range Olivier machines were status symbols for the fashionable rich. An 1867 advertisement listed 'velocipedes of enamelled, polished and damascened steel, polished or engraved aluminium-bronze. Wheels of West Indian hardwood, amaranth, makrussa, hickory, ebony or lemon tree. Handlebar grips of sculpted ivory. Especially created accessories: lanterns, pneumatic rubber saddles, flexible back-piece, luggage-carrier, grease-cups, patent pedals and pulley-operated brake.' The brake cord was tightened by the rider revolving the handlebar, to which it was fastened.

to accept a 200,000 francs pay-off and left the firm. In the five years up to 1867 an average of only 250 machines a year had been produced. In early 1870 the Olivier Brothers were boasting of 200 machines a day built by 500 workers using 57 forges. There were by this time around sixty other producers of velocipedes in Paris, and fifteen or so in the provinces.

In August 1869 Jules Suriray, Superintendent of Prisoners' Workshops, patented and produced ball-bearings for wheel-hubs. The balls, finely polished by Suriray's captive workforce, were used in the wheels of a number of top class steel racing machines in 1869. The best Olivier machines also used ball-bearings. Products on show at the Paris Velocipede Exhibition of 1869 included metal-spoked wheels, solid rubber tyres, a lever-operated four speed gear, a freewheel and mudguards. By the end of the 1860s the French velocipede industry was years ahead of any foreign competition, and full of confidence. 'The velocipedes we see around us', said the journalist Richard Lesclide, 'have more or less reached perfection.'[4]

The velocipede acquired vociferous friends and enemies. One of its most eloquent advocates was the same Richard Lesclide:

The velocipede is one step ahead on the road taken by the genius of Man. In place of collective speed—which is brutal and unthinking—it offers individualised speed: rapidity founded on the power of reason. It is able to circumvent obstacles, adapt to conditions, and is subject to the will of the rider.[5]

A writer for *Le Galois* was less enthusiastic, proclaiming that 'Velocipedists are imbeciles on wheels.' Doctors were particularly divided in their opinions. Some warned of headaches and hernias caused by road vibrations; others recommended the velocipede as a cure for obesity, gout, sluggish liver and dyspepsia. In his book *Hygiène du Vélocipède* Doctor Paraclèse Bellencontre predicted that the velocipede would contribute to 'the higher moralisation of the masses'. It would, he thought, improve family life by enabling working men from outlying districts to get back to their families each evening, rather than lodge near their workplace from Monday to Saturday and be tempted by the immorality of the city. He claimed that the velocipede would 'distract young people's attention from other passions and prevent them from abandoning themselves prematurely to the pleasures of love'. It would also help keep young men away from 'the dirty and unhygenic atmosphere ... of the tabacco saloon, bar and tavern'. It would make them into 'vigorous young lads with solid muscles—in other words, men, worthy of the French nation'.

Bellencontre's sonorous reformism was not furthered by the velocipede race meetings which took place in Paris and other cities. These events took on much of the paraphernalia of horse racing: track-side bets were placed on riders wearing jockey caps and jackets of variously coloured silk, and competing for purses and cups. Velocipedists were rather more versatile than horses and promoters spiced up the programme with slow 'races', no-handlebar races and gymnastic riding. Members of the royal family and aristocracy attended races in Paris, such as that organised by the Véloce-Club de Paris on the 17 June 1869, at which 10,000 spectators watched a total of 300 competitors on the grass of the Pré Catalan, to the music of a brass band.

The world's first successful cycling magazine was *Le Vélocipède Illustré*, first published on the 1 April 1869. It was mostly the work of the previously mentioned Richard Lesclide, supported by voluntary local correspondents. The tone was set by the opening words of the first issue: 'The velocipede is rapidly penetrating our moral outlook and our way of life ... One is no less a man for being a velocipedist. The French spirit, style and skill [as shown by velocipedists] have never come amiss.' Lesclide also responded to those who wanted velocipeding banned on the grounds of danger. By the same token, he wrote, locomotives should be banned since they catch fire and derail; cabs and horse-omnibuses should be banned since they are known to have killed 1211 people in 1867; and walking should be banned as pedestrians are exposed to the danger of sprained ankles, sunstroke and falling chimney pots. 'First came the Rights of Man', he wrote elsewhere, 'now let us secure the Rights of the Velocipede.'[6]

One amusing feature of this bi-weekly magazine was a serialised account of a round-the-world velocipede ride undertaken by Mr Jonathan Schopp, a fabulously rich and handsome American, and a 'noble republican'. His machine was the finest money could buy, and was the brainchild of his mentor, who was mysteriously known as 'the Napoleon of Velocipedes'. Schopp progressed heroically around the world, facing constant danger and covering superhuman distances. It was clearly fiction. But on the 22 April the following letter was published: 'Sir, Would you please give me the address of Jonathan Schopp or of the Napoleon of Velocipedes. I can be of great service to them since I am the inventor of a velocipede which will go at an unlimited speed.' On the 17 June came a letter from a reader living near the German border. He had, he said, followed the same route as Schopp through Germany. But how could the American possibly have covered the distance in the time mentioned, and on such awful roads? And how, asked the reader, had Schopp got on so well with the German peasantry when the reader himself had encountered nothing but hostility?

The *Vélocipède Illustré* joined forces with the Olivier Brothers' Compagnie Parisienne des Vélocipèdes to sponsor and organise the Paris–Rouen road race of the 9 November 1869. Between one and three hundred competitors (estimates vary) took part on two, three and four-wheeled machines. At least four women entered, and one of them, described as 'Miss America', came in 29th. The winner was James Moore, an Englishman living in Paris. His average speed for the 123 kilometres was 12 k.p.h. (7½ m.p.h.). His machine had a large front wheel and used Suriray's ball-bearings.

In French road racing events women could compete against men. In track races, before paying spectators, they were equally welcome but usually raced in their own events at the end of the programme. The organisers' motives were probably more commercial than egalitarian: the mixing of athleticism and femininity seems to have been a major voyeuristic attraction to male customers, and a boon to profits. There are few clues to the social background of the *vélocipèdeuses*. Some may have been hired actresses, and others recruited from the several troupes of velocipede acrobats who performed in Paris and on tour. Some may well have been independent-minded daughters of the bourgeoisie. Articles in the *Vélocipède Illustré* on competition-wear for women suggest a sizeable middle-class female readership who, at least occasionally, rode on the track. The question of women's social background is obscured by male journalists who chose to associate plain, practical clothing with disreputable exhibitionism. A *Vélocipède Illustré* writer urged that lady competitors' clothing be based on *la fantaisie*. He suggested a Russian helmet-style hat topped with a long plume, a lined or braided doublet and lace pantaloons, knee-length and loose. The latter were not so much a concession to liberalism as a necessity: longer garments would entangle in the wheels.[7]

Non-competitive velocipeding became popular among 'respectable' ladies. There was a ladies' riding hall inside the velocipede school of the Compagnie Parisienne, and *grandes dames* could often be seen pedalling off the main thoroughfares. And Jonathan Schopp, weary of circumvelocipeding the globe in manly isolation, welcomes the company of a lady velocipedist who joins him on his travels. It is stressed that the relationship remains at all times founded on innocent and honourable friendship.

A passionate supporter of velocipeding for women was Paraclèse Bellencontre, official doctor of the Véloce-Club de Rouen. In his previously mentioned book, *Hygiène du Vélocipède*, he contrasts the advantages of velocipeding with the moral dangers of dancing. For, when dancing,

> habitually naked shoulders become covered in sweat, affording open and undefended passage to all pulmonary and catarrhal infections. The waist is locked into its tight prison of gauze, satin and flowers, and the respira-

21 Sprinting to the finish in a race at Bordeaux in November 1868. Another version of this sketch has the women's legs covered to the knees.

tory system fails to furnish the body with blood, being troubled by the air fouled by the flames of the chandeliers and by personal emanations ... [However] a velocipede, be it ever so flighty, would never encourage our mothers, sisters and daughters to wear those scanty dresses of flimsy transparent material ... designed to entice the male dancing partner looking down.

Bellencontre further warns that during intimate waltzes a young girl might plan with her partner ways of giving her mother the slip. None of this can happen on a velocipede, he asserts, since velocipeding couples need to keep well away from each other to avoid collisions. He recommends that velocipeding become an important part of girls' formal education, and that it be used in the treatment of 'pale, anaemic girls with a tendency to scrofula, and those for whom the onset of menstruation is proving difficult'.

While society debated the implications of the machine Pierre Michaux continued to refine his product. He introduced an improved rear brake and bronze pedals which were weighted to remain horizontal. He also developed an axle for quickly converting a two-wheeled Michauline into a tricycle. Michaux may have regretted his decision to sell out completely to the Olivier Brothers in late 1869 or 1870, for he set up a new manufactory in his own name and in direct competition with them. This being a breach of the severence contract, they sued him and won damages of 100,000 francs. Ruined by legal costs, damages and the onset of war, Michaux died in a paupers' hospice in Paris in 1883.

The Franco-Prussian War broke out quite suddenly and unexpectedly in July 1870, and the French velocipede industry vanished in the turmoil. France was heavily defeated. Paris was besieged, shelled and starved; and after capitulation came the massacres of the Commune.

Before the great collapse an enthusiasm for velocipeding had been spread abroad. In 1868 J. T. Scholte of the Dutch Metalwork Factory was advertising that he had sought out and copied the best Parisian machines and could offer them at half of Paris prices. Amsterdam took well to the velocipede, but riders who pioneered into the Dutch countryside often met with a boorish resentment which was to weaken little in three decades (and contrasting sharply with that country's present attitude to cycling). Charles Boissevain, former editor of the *Algemeen Handelsblad*, recalled that 'between Diemerbrug and Amsterdam I had such a hefty lump of coal thrown at my front wheel that the wheel broke. It had been thrown with full force by a fellow on a passing tow-boat, and I have to be thankful that the impassioned perpetrator missed my head.'[8]

Velocipede races became highly popular in Belgium. A race in Ghent failed to take place because the size of the crowd left the riders no room. In Germany velocipeding frequently met with organised resistance. When riders first took to the streets of Bremen, in March 1869, they were surrounded by a menacing mob and only just escaped. Thereupon, a group of local notables stormed into the town hall and demanded that velocipeding be prohibited. The council banned the activity within an eight kilometre (five-mile) radius of the city. A similar ban, of seven kilometres, was already in force in Berlin. None of the many German anti-velocipeding measures inconvenienced Jonathan Schopp, for he carried in his pocket a letter from his close friend, Bismark, authorising him to ride where he wished. The city of Vienna, always receptive to French fashions, was enthusiastic: in 1869 there were three indoor riding schools and numerous race grounds. In Switzerland the principal cities had velocipede clubs by 1869. Club-organised road races consisted at first of short sprints, but the state of the roads made the more leisurely 20 to 25 kilometre *course de voyage* a more acceptable event. A *Vélocipède Illustré* correspondent from Berne reported in June 1869 that tricycles were becoming popular in the area, and tricyclists were gaining the upper hand in long distance events and hill-climbing.

The American Enthusiasm

In 1866 Pierre Lallement emigrated from Paris to the United States and, together with a new-found business partner, James Carroll, took out a patent for a Michaux-style velocipede.[9] The first velocipedes to leave their workshops in New Haven, Connecticut, were widely ridiculed, as were subsequently redesigned machines. Disappointed, Lallement returned to France and set up in belated and unsuccessful competition with Pierre Michaux. Back in America news of the velociped ing phenomenon in Paris was being reported by magazines and returning tourists. There developed a demand for velocipedes which was responded to quickly and prodigiously by American manufacturers, unmindful of the luckless Lallement's patent rights. By 1867 nuts and bolts were being tightened for a 'velocipedomania' which was to rival, if not surpass, that of Paris.

The great impresarios of the new enthusiasm were the Hanlon Brothers, celebrated acrobats and entertainers. They promoted exuberant exhibitions of velocipede gymnastics, with themselves top of the bill. Their touring show, the *Hanlon Superba*, featured fancy-dress riding and speed demonstrations, all to the sound of energetic music. Their shows created a demand for velocipedes which the brothers themselves helped meet; they became not only major manufacturers, but also owners of the largest velocipede hall in New York City.

The craze was most intense in New York, Boston and New Haven.

Outdoor riding was not feasible in Winter and any large hall was liable to become a rink or riding school. Ballrooms, meeting rooms, attics and even a church vestry were pressed into service. The Sommerville Art Gallery on New York's Fifth Avenue became a ladies' riding school, and the New York Velocipede Academy was set up in the former regimental armoury. Boston's Horticultural Hall became the most elegant of the city's twenty velociping venues, and adjoining Cambridge had the largest velociping hall in the country with an area of 12,000 square feet. But many establishments were impromptu affairs: 'The old church on the corner of State and Court sts was turned into a riding-room and beginners were "at it" night and day, for the span of a week. The shopkeepers below objected to having the plaster from the walls sprinkled upon them, and so the rink was closed.'[10]

The names of the halls matched the dilirium of the time: *velocipedarium, velocinasium, gymnacyclidium, amphicyclotheatron.* Instructors were *professors of the velocipede* or *velocipedagogues*. The major halls were constantly busy. Customers would bring or hire machines in the daytime; evenings were commonly set aside for entertainments such as acrobatics by 'Parisian' artistes, velocipede cavalry drill, 'tag' riding and obstacle races. A regular and leading rink exhibitionist was Charles A. Dana, the velocipede-obsessed editor of the New York *Sun*. Prize races were also introduced but proved so dangerous that they were replaced by individual rides against the clock.

Over the Winter of 1868–9 riding schools were gorged with pupils. According to a contemporary source New York had some 10,000 pupils and Boston had nearly the same number. In Philadelphia, Chicago, St Louis and San Francisco experts could be counted in hundreds and novices in thousands. There was a general excitement. On the 9 January the *Scientific American* declared that 'for the majority of civilised humanity, walking is on its last legs', and the writer of a velocipede manual wrote:

> We play velocipede music, and in our walks velocipede 'Livery Stables' and 'Velocipedes to Let' greet our eyes. The shop-windows on our fashionable thoroughfares display Velocipede Hats, Velocipede Gloves and Velocipede Shoes.[11]

Those unwilling or unable to buy a machine could watch performing velocipedists on the public squares, and had a choice of entertainments in the halls. There were also the new inventions to marvel at, either directly or through the 'Velocipede Notes' in the press. For twenty-five cents you could see 'the only steam velocipede in the world', as exhibited by the owner, Sylvester H. Roper, on Broadway, New York. It could 'be driven up any hill', and could 'out-speed any horse in the world'.

22 A scene from a riding-school on Broadway, New York City. Pupils paid fifteen dollars a months for their pleasure.

American velocipedes varied greatly in quality. Some, made of cast iron, were perilous and quickly abandoned. One of the best and most popular makes was the Pickering and Davis, which had frame and forks made of steel tubing, and readily replaceable parts. Some of these models had a brake attached to the back of the saddle. By pushing against the handlebars the rider forced the saddle backwards, pushing the brake down onto the rear wheel. Velocipedes could also be made by amateurs using plans published in technical magazines. Wooden wheels for this purpose could be bought ready-made and in fourteen different sizes from a firm in Chicago. Machines were usually finished in bright colours, and often with bold carriage-livery stripes.

A somewhat farcical velocipede patent dispute broke out. A New York manufacturer, Calvin Witty, discovered Lallement's neglected design patent and bought all rights from him. He then informed the twenty or so major manufacturers that they were infringing his patent and demanded a ten dollar royalty on every machine sold in the USA. Many firms obliged

43

and others took out expensive law suits with varying results. The wily Witty was himself sued, unsuccessfully, by Stephen W. Smith, who claimed that he had, in 1862, patented the original velocipede and had even been the one who first introduced it to France. Branding Lallement's patent 'a palpable piracy of my rights', Smith demanded ten dollars (but sometimes five dollars after negotiation) on each machine sold. His patent turned out to have been bought from a P. W. MacKenzie and was for a 'cantering propeller': a preposterous pedal-less rocking horse on two wheels.

Religious authorities pondered the moral implications of velocipeding. Should one, for example, velocipede to church or to a funeral? Henry Ward Beecher, the celebrated pastor of the Plymouth Congregational Church of Brooklyn, hoped to see 'a thousand velocipedists wheeling [i.e. riding] their machines to Plymouth Church'. At the other extreme was the case of a youth from a religiously conservative Shaker community who made his own velocipede. His father maintained that such a machine could be ridden only towards the devil and smashed it with an axe. The boy left home.[12]

Newspapers were sometimes critical, especially if their readerships were well away from the heartland of the velocipede vogue. The *Detroit Post* expressed contempt at seeing anyone who 'looks as though he ought to be out chopping wood, straddling a two-wheeled toy in the middle of the day' (31 March 1869). Another newspaper asserted that 'to see a grown man, tolerably well formed, on top of a hoop, and a crowd of boys, black and white, after him, is very pitiful . . . We prefer to see our young men handling, and learning to handle, the hoe.'[13]

As spring approached, the inmates of the rinks became eager for the open road. Outings and tours were planned, accessories such as lunchboxes and lanterns were bought, and columnists advised the fitting of mudguards. Rink owners looked forward to a lively trade in hire-outs, which would not be limited by the size of their rinks; and a form of velocipede 'livery stable' opened up at the entrance to Central Park. Soon riders were swarming onto the roads. On the 3 May the *New York Times* reported 'quantities of velocipedes flying like shuttles hither and thither'. This enthusiasm did not last long, as the lamentable road surfaces took their toll on machines and riders. There were no asphalted roads in New York, and probably none in other cities. For many riders, accustomed only to the smooth boards of riding halls, the roads supplied some rude shocks. Sidewalk riding increased, until pedestrian protest led to legislation against it, and velocipedists were additionally banned from Central Park. There appears to have been little wish to return to the rinks, for rink owners were forced to reduce their prices drastically. Some reduced their standards, bringing in second-rate display riding by disreputably dressed women. By the end of April velocipeding was being diagnosed as moribund and by August very few respectable citizens were still riding. Some of the New York halls had become the resort of 'roughs', who monopolised the floors. Both manufacturers and the owners of riding halls and rinks suffered badly.

Velocipedes in Britain

British interest in velociping was less frenzied and more durable than had been the case in France or the United States. The earliest known British imitator of Michaux was a Finsbury Market scale-maker, Edward Norrington, who was making velocipedes in 1864. Only after 1867, the year in which velocipedes caught the attention of English visitors to the Paris Exhibition, were machines produced in significant quantities, and in the industrial Midlands rather than London. Many were produced speculatively, as an adjunct to an existing business. Of the sixteen velocipede makers active in Birmingham in 1870, four were additionally machine engineers, three were gunsmiths and two made sewing machines. The others' specialisms were: rivet maker, diesinker, coachsmith, axletree maker, furniture maker, fishing reel manufacturer (and one unknown). One of the ten velocipede makers in neighbouring Wolverhampton was Henry Clarke, a

23 Two-wheeled velocipedes lessened the popularity of their four-wheeled predecessors. However, this British oddity combined both species, and was probably made from two separate machines. The spokes of the front wheel are most unusual.

maker of carriages and perambulator wheels, who had been exporting velocipede wheels to France in 1867–68. Clarke's interest was long-standing. In the 1850s he and a friend had reputedly built a tandem tricycle which they rode around Wolverhampton 'amid the laughter and astonishment of the natives'.[14]

Nottingham's first velocipedes were imported from France by James Northage, owner of a brush and basket shop. He had seen them at the Paris Exhibition and ordered about six. In 1868 he set up a riding school in a long room over some carriage houses, having brought over from Paris 'Professor' Jules Larue, an instructor who claimed (as did most in that profession) to have taught the Prince Imperial. Northage began to manufacture in a small way but demand was light. It was also in Nottingham that Thomas Humber, of later bicycle and motor fame, began making velocipedes, after failing to find work at Northage's factory.[15]

By 1869 bigger firms had become involved, such as Newton, Wilson and Co., sewing machine manufacturers of London and Birmingham. Tangyes of Smethwick, a famous hydraulic engineering concern, built large numbers of velocipedes at their Cornwall works, paying royalties to France (very probably to the Compagnie Parisienne). There is a tale that Joseph Tangye made a velocipede with metal rather than wooden rims, and that this inventiveness was quashed by his brother James who stipulated 'no more toys!' However, it was the sustained inventiveness of Coventry manufacturers which ensured the long-term development and international popularity of British-made cycles, and made Coventry the cycle capital of the world.

There was, again, a Parisian connection. The Coventry Sewing Machine Company had an agent in Paris: Rowley Turner, the manager's nephew. Turner was seized by the velocipede mania and became an expert practitioner. In partnership with a gymnasium proprietor he put money into the building of a riding school with stores and workshops. The business blossomed. Late in 1868 he took a velocipede over to Coventry and persuaded his uncle's company to take up their manufacture. As the first batch were being produced the firm fittingly changed its name to the 'Coventry Machinists' Company'. All went well until their market was swept away by the Franco-Prussian War of 1870, but the demand was more than taken up by home sales. Their talented works-foreman, James Starley, left in 1869, but his inventive genius, evident before and after his move, helped give Coventry and ultimately the whole British cycle industry, a decisive lead and an appreciative long-term market.

'Extraordinary Velocipede Feat' was how *The Times* proclaimed a day-ride from London to Brighton on the 17 February 1869 by John Mayall, Charles Spencer and Rowley Turner (of Coventry Machinists connections). After circuiting Trafalgar Square they set off accompanied by a *Times*

24 John Mayall, who rode from London to Brighton in February 1869 on a Coventry Machinists' velocipede.

reporter in a coach and pair. Mayall arrived long before the others.[16] His performance—fifty-three miles in about fifteen hours—was hardly outstanding, and he could, perhaps, have walked it faster. Indeed, the brothers Chinnery of the London Stock Exchange walked the same route about 3½ hours faster the following month. Nevertheless, Mayall's achievement pointed to the fascinating possibility of velocipede-touring.

47

Liverpool velocipedists had no need to wait for machines from Midlands factories. Pickering and Davis velocipedes were imported into the city from the United States, and became the standard mount of the Liverpool Velocipede Club, founded in 1867. This first British club flourished. In April 1869 it held a public 'bicycle tournament' in a large gymnasium. The events, directed by a Mr Anderson, 'Master of Arms', included tilting at rings, throwing the javelin, fencing, drilled evolutions and fancy riding.

There was a growing interest in road riding and touring. In March 1869 two members of the Liverpool Velocipede Club rode from Liverpool to London in a remarkable three days. *The Times* of the 31 March reported that:

> their bicycles caused no little astonishment on the way, and the remarks passed by the natives were almost amusing. At some of the villages the boys clustered round the machines, and, where they could, caught hold of them and ran behind until they were tired out. Many enquiries were made

25 One of the events at the Liverpool Velocipede Club's bicycle tournament of April 1869.

as to the name of 'them queer horses', some called them 'whirligigs', 'menageries' and 'valparaisos'. Between Wolverhampton and Birmingham, attempts were made to upset the riders by throwing stones.

The interest in touring was reflected in the literature of the time. In *Wheels and Woes*, written by 'a Light Dragoon' in 1870 or 1871, there is advice on how to go about it:

> Once a rider finds it necessary every time he goes out to gird on gaiters, belts, leather-patched trousers and lamp, the B. becomes a bore ... For persons travelling in winter time, when night comes on so fast, a lamp is very advisable ... as a preventative against being mummified by a market cart, or hashed up by some hasty horseman. Those who have any experience of the bucolic mind, particularly when in charge of market carts after dark, must have remarked its very strong tendency to appropriate the wrong side of the road whenever it is possible to do so ... The French plan is to carry a 'Bull's eye,' *à la Beaubie*, on a belt, in front of the body. If you don't wear a lamp then don a little bell like a sheep tinkler. Some Bicycles *are* made with bells attached to the pedals; or if you are musically inclined, why not a whole ring of bells along the Governor? ... By moonlight there is nothing so charming as a turn on the wheels, always excepting, *bien entendu*, a stroll in certain company—*Place aux dames*.

The book includes one of the earliest cycling travelogues, describing the author's ride from Lewes to Salisbury. It seems to have been a delightful adventure, despite bad road surfaces, dust and a lack of signposts.

As velocipedes were expensive, owners tended to be single and middle-class males: clerks, tradesmen, engineers, teachers, and young men of private means. Prince Leopold, youngest son of Queen Victoria, was also a rider, as were many public schoolboys. According to the 'Light Dragoon' velocipeding was banned at Eton, partly because it allowed the boys to wander out of bounds so easily, and partly because of their attempts at 'the practice of steeple-chasing!—ditches almost 15 inches in width, and raspers nearly 10 inches in height, being rushed at, and, I need not add, cleared, regardless of croppers or broken cranks, by the budding, sporting pluck of England.'

As in other countries there was a reaction against velocipeding and against anti-social riding in particular. According to the Manchester *Sphynx* of April 1869, 'if babies want to be wheeled along the footpath they must go in perambulators, and not on velocipedes.' There were pleas for self-regulation. The author of *Velocipedes of the Period*, an 1869 manual for riders, urged severity against over-fast riders:

Let it be understood that, in every case of conviction, the penalty will be imprisonment without the option of a fine. Possibly a few days' use of the stationary velocipede at Coldbath Fields [a prison treadmill] may assist such ardent velocipedists to acquire the art of performing the crank and pedal motion to slower time.

Local races took place in fields, with no great regard for accurate timing or measurement. One of the earliest events was held in May 1868, on a field behind the Welsh Harp Hotel (public house) in Hendon. The winner, Arthur Markham, won a silver cup presented by the hotel's landlord. Occasionally a velocipede race would be included in a pedestrian meet. (Pedestrianism was a distinct sport: an early, loosely regulated form of athletics.) The Richmond Football Club introduced a velocipede event at its Autumn sports day in 1868 and regular races were held at the Crystal Palace. They were dominated by riders from France.

The demands of athletes and tourists induced manufacturers to develop lighter machines with larger front wheels and smaller rear ones, reflecting similar but more advanced developments in France which were cut short in 1870. The wooden-wheeled boneshaker was evolving into the imposing steel-wheeled high bicycle, since nicknamed the 'penny-farthing'.

26 The 'boneshaker' technology, of solid tyres and front-wheel cranks, was long applied to children's tricycles, and is still common today.

3
RIDING THE HIGH WHEEL

The high-riding Clubmen

IN 1882, A MERE FOURTEEN YEARS after the foundation of the British cycle industry, a 'monster meet' of bicyclists was held at Hampton Court Palace near London. Sitting above wheels almost the height of a standing man, 2177 riders formed a colourful but ceremonious procession six miles in length. They paraded around the grounds, club after club, each distinguishable by its uniform, apart from some provincial clubs which had ridden from afar and were anonymously caked in road dust.[1] The Hampton meets had been growing in importance since the first in 1876. They were not only displays of finery, riding skill and discipline, but also an affirmation of solidarity, and public evidence that bicyclists were both respectable and numerous.

27 The Pickwick Bicycle Club leads the parade at Hampton Court in 1877.

The wheelmen's increasing sense of social importance was matched, and even encouraged, by the increased size of their bicycles. High bicycles, later to be known as penny-farthings, were reaching the peak of refinement in that year of 1882: the front wheel had become as big as the rider's leg length would allow, giving more distance per revolution and a more comfortable ride over rough roads. Wheels were being made of steel, had hollow-section rims, and were strengthened by new spoking techniques. Hollow tubing was lightening frames and forks; the average bicycle would weigh about forty-five pounds and a competitive machine about twenty pounds. Direct-drive, a minimal backbone and solid rubber tyres made bicycles elegantly simple. There was little to go wrong and only problems such as a cracked frame or rim would require a visit to the blacksmith.

The high bicycle was never safe. For maximum pedalling efficiency the rider sat almost directly above the straight front forks, always in danger of being pitched forward, an event known as a 'cropper', 'header' or 'imperial crowner'. Going downhill some riders slung their legs over the handlebar, hoping to be pitched clear should the front wheel hit a pothole, awkward stone or straying farmyard beast. As there was no freewheel mechanism the rider could slow himself down by back-pressure on the pedals, an opportunity which was lost when wheeling downhill with feet up and pedals whirring out of control. There was also usually a small lever-operated spoon brake which, if too effective, could itself cause a cropper. Even misjudged back-pedalling could send a man over the top. On the other hand riders could claim a strong sense of intimacy with their machines thanks to the proximity of the front wheel, the control of that wheel through back as well as forward pressure, and the functional simplicity of the machine as a whole.

So demanding was the high bicycle that it appealed to athletic and adventurous males who found pleasure in sharing the sense of risk with fellow clubmen, and in mastering the fastest vehicle on the roads. And if personal status was sometimes associated with the height of a rider's wheel, it was an infinitely more innocent failing than the later forms of self-aggrandisement through fast motor cars. Communal bravado and mutual admiration were not the only reasons for joining a bicycle club. Riding in a club gave some protection against the ridicule, insults and stones which were sometimes aimed at wheelmen.

Most clubmen were middle-class town or city people, and they were exclusively male. The pastime was considered too dangerous for women, and long skirts made it impossible for them. The upper classes preferred their own, less controversial, pastimes such as boating, tennis, riding, polo and carriage outings. Working-class men would have been hard put to afford twelve pounds for a bicycle and a further three or four pounds for a uniform and club fees. The sport was democratised just a little after about 1882 by lower bicycle prices, a growing second-hand market, and the willingness of a few clubs to hire out bicycles. The choice of Saturday for club runs handicapped the many working-class men who worked all that day, although a good number of clubs had Saturday afternoon rides for those whose work was over by mid-day. Sunday riding was frowned upon by the Church of England and by the Lord's Day Observance Society. Club rules often disallowed the wearing of uniforms and club badges on a Sunday, and runs tended to be unofficial. Riders often referred to such outings as 'church parades', perhaps to draw a humorous contrast between ecclesiastical and cycling activities, but possibly in reference to the large number of churches which a rider would pass on a day run. The Cyclists' Touring Club requested members who rode on a Sunday to remove or cover-up their CTC badges. Since Saturday work and Sunday observance were so prevalent, many clubs held evening rides.

Bicyclists tended to be young, for social as well as physical reasons. The Rev. Mr Courtney, himself an ardent cyclist, wrote: 'When men pass a certain age, say five-and-thirty, they have generally made such a position in life that they cannot, without endangering their dignity, join a club comprising of young clerks and other men of business, however good the social position of the parents of these juvenile clubmen may be.' (*The Cyclist*, 24 Dec. 1879)

The club uniform was typically dark in colour and consisted of a pill-box hat with the club badge attached, a short, wool-lined, brass-buttoned jacket, tight breeches and stout riding shoes. The bugler was additionally enhanced with massive tasselled cord. The club captain could be identified by such items as gold braiding or a gilt badge, and the sub-captain wore the equivalent in silver. American clubs first copied British club customs but many switched to regular military titles, such as first and second lieutenant, and even committee posts were militarised. Also, American club bugle calls were taken directly from the *Cavalry Tactics Manual* of the US Army.[2]

Just as velocipede clubs had been a primarily French phenomenon of the 1860s, bicycle clubs were a predominantly British one of the 1870s and 1880s. One of the earliest clubs was the Pickwick. The minutes of its first meeting, in June 1870, contain a proposal that the club uniform consist of no more than a white straw hat with a black and amber ribbon: an informal precursor of the tassels, braid and badges of later clubs.[3] Another unmilitary aspect of the Pickwick Bicycle Club was the adoption by members of the names of characters from Dickens's *Pickwick Papers*, the whole amusement being based on the erroneous belief that Dickens rode a velocipede. By 1874 there were around 29 British clubs; by 1878 there were 189, and by 1882 there were 528, of which 199 were in the London area. An average club might have thirty members.

Club runs mixed formality with fun. High streets and market places up

28 The Christchurch Bicycle Club in 1879. The captain was, unusually, also the bugler. By 1883 the club had become 'decadent', having very few active riders.

and down the country would echo to the rumblings of bicycles on cobblestones as riders arrived for the 'off'. At the bugle call for 'assembly' the captain would take his place at the head of the riders, with the sub-captain at the rear. At the call for 'mount' each man in turn would put one foot on the mounting step by his rear wheel, hop along behind his machine, and then project himself up and forward into the saddle. A bugle blast for single file would gather the men together as they wheeled through sleepy streets, past bemused townspeople and bewildered horses, to surge out into a serene countryside with only occasional horse traffic. Once on the open road the bugler would call for 'double file', at which the riders could relax and chat, powering their great wheels along in a rhythm unbroken by freewheeling or gear changes. Conversation would be punctuated by bugle blasts intended to warn others of the club's approach. Villagers out for a walk no doubt stepped well back against the hedge, eyeing warily such a parody of a foxhunt. The clubmen would pass abandoned tollhouses before rattling along turnpike roads which had been little used, and badly neglected, since the arrival of the railways. The bicycle clubs brought new prosperity to many country inns which had not seen such custom since the days of the stage coach. After carefully stacking their machines the clubmen would go in for a drink to take the dust out of their mouths and perhaps tuck into a 'capital repast' or a 'cold collation'. This might be followed by solo renditions of popular songs, rounded off with the club anthem. Any tiredness on the homeward leg would be greatly worsened by a wind. So high was the profile of rider and machine that sidewinds brought steering problems and headwinds could force a rider to walk his machine home. As darkness fell each rider would dismount to light the oil lamp which hung from his handlebar or, more typically, from the hub inside the spokes of the front wheel. Slowly and carefully, peering for potholes, the clubmen would return to the commonplaces of town or city life.

A key event in the club's calendar was the 'meet'. A club would invite neighbouring clubs to gather for a parade, usually along the host town's bunting-hung high street, followed by a formal reception and entertainments in the clubhouse. Grander 'monster meets' were convened by clubs in large conurbations. In 1882 the Midlands Meet attracted 228 riders, the Glasgow Meet 273, and the Liverpool Meet 500. These monster meets offered extra amusements. The 1885 Midlands Meet was enlivened by fireworks, a balloon ascent and a race on static bicycles (the predecessors of our 'home-trainers'). The Lake District Meet of the same year offered a four-in-hand coach drive around Derwentwater. This latter monster meet was centred in Keswick, which was anything but a large conurbation. It was made possible by the railway companies, who offered excursion tickets for the purpose, and even laid on 'special through vans' for travellers' bicycles. A good turn-out of members at a meet was a matter of honour for clubs, as evidenced by a fastidious report on the Hampton Court Meet which appeared in *The Cyclist* of the 24 May 1882. Not content with having counted the riders with his 'American Automatic Enumerator', the correspondent listed each club together with the number of riders it had present, all followed by a corrective article the following week with minute adjustments to the figures.

Bicyclists were very much at the mercy of the public and of professional carters in particular, who had been long accustomed to empty roads. In 1876 the driver of the Watford to St Albans coach lashed an overtaking bicyclist with his whip, and his conductor brought down a following bicyclist by flinging an iron ball attached to a rope into his spokes. Their actions led to a test case in court: 'The magistrates sat in a small room which was filled with bicyclists and coaching people, all of whom listened to the proceedings with great interest, and frequently gave vent to their feelings by stamping, hissing, and what almost amounted to cheering.' (*The Bicycle Journal*, 8 Sept. 1876.) Parsons, the driver, was fined £2 and Cracknall, the conductor, £5. 'We think to charge £5 for the chance of killing a man is holding human life too cheap', remarked the same journal. Two years later the rights of cyclists were improved by the Highways and Locomotives (Amendment) Act, which clarified the bicycle's legal status, but it left the matter of cycling-related bye-laws to local councils.

Victorian wheelmen had at least one advantage over modern cyclists: they could out-pace and overhaul horse-drawn culprits. After a cab driver tried to run down three cyclists near Long Ditton they chased him to Surbiton

29 Hilaire Belloc, aged about seventeen. Two years later, in 1889, he toured provincial France as a correspondent for the *Pall Mall Gazette*, and bought a high bicycle for the purpose.

and brought him to justice. The solo rider was more vulnerable:

> During the ride through Somerton to Glastonbury I became the victim
> first of stupidity, then of malice. A waggoner seeing me about to overtake
> him pulled very suddenly over to the wrong side, and sent me sprawling
> over a heap of flints. No harm done. Shortly afterwards a wilful misdirec-
> tion given me by a playful Sumertonian sent me 2½ miles in the wrong
> direction.[4]

Another human hazard was the over-zealous policeman. Few bicyclists
were completely safe from a summons for 'furious riding' since police
evidence could only ever be impressionistic. *The Cyclist* of the 1 November
1882 reported how a gentleman of 'a most respectable address' was prose-
cuted for riding in London at an alleged 10 m.p.h. The magazine was
indignant: 'Our readers know from statistics . . . published in our columns at
what pace the traffic along the Kensington Road travels, and that if 10 miles
an hour is "furious driving", half the hansoms in London should be daily
summoned for the offence.' The cyclist concerned was fined the maximum
of forty shillings by the magistrate, John Paget, the wheelmen's *bête noire*.
They maintained that he always believed the police account and always
imposed the maximum fine. An extreme example of police malpractice
occurred near Warrington in 1882. A constable grounded a footpath-riding
cyclist by pushing his truncheon into his spokes. Having been fined for his
own offence the cyclist claimed and received damages against the policeman.
On reporting this case *The Cyclist* of the 3 May 1882 remarked: 'Bicyclists
are mostly young men with their position yet to gain, but they will some day
be ratepayers, and acts of injustice are apt to rankle in the mind longer than
any other feeling.' The implication was that, as ratepayers, they would hold
influence over the rate-funded police force, whose status was low at the
time. There were, no doubt, some inconsiderate wheelmen, who frightened
horses and endangered pedestrians. Cycling magazines and figures of authority expressed concern at such bad publicity for their cause. In April
1882 *The Cyclist* urged moderation:

> The coaching season on roads out of London commences for the Summer
> this month . . . We trust that bicyclists will remember that they can easily
> beat a four-in-hand coach if they try, and that they will rest content at
> that, and not bring odium upon our sport by trying to race coaches, as the
> 'buzzing about' of bicycles causes much trouble to coachmen, amateur
> and professional.

On the 31 May 1885 *The Cyclist*'s 'own correspondent' in Cambridge
wrote:

I regret that the cheap rate at which a large number of 'second-hand' machines have recently been disposed of has placed two-wheelers in the hands of the dangerous hobbledehoy class, whose mad careerings in the public streets are rapidly rendering cycling a complete nuisance. Several accidents have recently occured owing to the mischievous proclivities of these 'butterfly riders'.

And one curious case of conflict in Birmingham was reported in *The Warcry*, the organ of the Salvation Army: 'A slave of the enemy on a bicycle tried to ride through our ranks, but the Lord upset him and he fell on his head.'[5]

The club system helped to curb the excesses of individual members, but sometimes it was the corporate enthusiasm of the club itself which caused problems. The very extravagance of clubmen's behaviour and apparel provided a distinctive, if moving target, for resentful ridicule. Rural Britain, in the slough of an agricultural depression, did not always take kindly to the intrusion of excited young men from the towns, whose machines seemed bizarre, whose uniforms could be hurtfully compared to the gaudy garb of a German band, and whose bugle calls, if not expertly blown, could bring derision rather than respect.

Some club riding took the form of long tours, especially at Easter. These tours often involved men and machines taking to the railways for stretches of the route: the extensive rail network complemented the bicycle extremely well. A club's home-based cycling activities might include paper-chases, novelty events at local sports days, moonlight rides in Winter and Chinese lantern rides in Summer. For the latter event the clubmen festooned their machines with paper lanterns. Very few roads remained rideable beyond October and clubs kept their members together by a programme of non-cycling activities: smoking concerts, dinners, *soirées dansantes*, boxing and billiard tournaments, and 'assaults at arms', which were a form of athletics tournament first popularised by the Canonbury Bicycle Club. In 1881 the Lewisham Bicycle Club organised an assault at arms for which 1000 men filled the New Cross Hall. There was boxing, fencing, quarterstaffing, 'ancient combat', parallel bar feats, wrestling, a sword and bayonet competition and a tug of war.[6]

The clubhouse or clubrooms were a home from home for many members. A newly established club would hire a room in an inn or above a shop. In time some could afford their own clubhouse, but often only by enrolling new members so as to keep up funds. Some clubs became so ensconced in their comfortable clubhouses that they turned out fewer and fewer riders for runs. They simply metamorphosed into men's social clubs. One such 'bogus' or 'decadent' club was bitterly criticised in *The Cyclist* of the 4

30 Goy's, the sports out-fitters, of Lime Street, London.

October 1882. This (unnamed) South Coast club, with a membership of nearly a hundred, turned out only three members for its own annual meet. A Temperance Movement speaker at the club's annual dinner praised its 'laudable endeavours to keep young men out of public-house bars', and yet the balance sheets showed that the club survived on profits from alcohol sales and billiard table receipts. It had also become a regular gambling den. As the Bournemouth Bicycle and Tricycle Club defended itself the cap was thought to have fitted and, on the 1 November 1882, *The Cyclist* attacked this club specifically, complaining of low riding activity despite a sudden quadrupling of the membership, and failure to wear correct uniforms. And there had been a card game scandal after which two members were called upon to resign and shortly afterwards left town. Such club 'decadence' was common on the South Coast. In his book, *Victorian High-Wheelers*, Roger T. C. Street describes how the Christchurch Bicycle Club, which was founded in 1876, had become essentially a billiards club by 1883. Billiards was regarded as a high-class game at the time. The fund for building a club race track was used to buy a new billiards table for an astonishing eighty-five guineas. One contributory reason for this decline, he suggests, may have been boredom with the limited number of routes available for day-outings. Not all clubs declined and vigorous new ones came along, although after about 1885 there was less interest in public displays of splendour. In 1886 one clubman wrote that an unusually large meet of that year 'forcibly reminded [him] of the palmy days when club musters were large and regular'.[7]

Cyclists who had the time and money for regular touring, and who preferred to avoid local clubs, could join the Bicycle Touring Club, although many belonged to both. The Bicycle Touring Club was founded in Harrogate in 1878 and renamed the Cyclists' Touring Club in 1883. This national club, whose membership rose from 836 in 1879 to 22,316 in 1886, sought to safeguard cyclists' interests in general. It undertook test case prosecutions, published a gazette and arranged favourable hotel tariffs for members. In 1882 there were 773 appointed hotels, many with a lounge for the sole use of club members. There was also a recommended BTC/CTC uniform, which was subject to frequent (and expensive) changes of colour. The initial green uniforms were found to show the dirt. Lilac or heather-grey came next, followed by iron-grey, then brown. In 1884 the iron-grey uniform cost £3. 19s. 6d. CTC members were generally a respectable lot, and odd *Gazette* items about members' 'delinquencies' brought appeals from correspondents for a raising of the annual subscription from 2/6 to 5/-, so as to squeeze out undesirables.

Cycling magazines carried news of products, personalities, events and tours which would otherwise have been left to word of mouth. They provided a forum for readers. There were moral questions to discuss, such as whether one was entitled to box the ears of a boy who had tried to cause one a cropper. Was pavement riding permissible if there were no pedestrians in sight? There were opinions on products. One reader reported that his 'Anti-pluvium macintosh suit' did not let out the sweat, while another found that his 'Swan and Edgar's sun-cured gossamer suit' was quite ideal. There was medical advice. *The Cyclist* of the 24 August 1881 advised that sunstroke could be avoided by 'putting a cabbage leaf in the crown of the polo or other headgear'. Sufferers from heatstroke should be 'put under a pump and pumped on'. There was also a preventative for sore feet: 'A raw egg, broken inside the shoe before putting it on, is said to soften the leather.' Alternatively the shoe could be doused in whisky. The cure for foot blisters was to 'take off the shoes and change stockings . . . or, if only one foot hurts, take off the shoe and turn the stocking inside out. These plans were adopted by Captain Barclay, the celebrated pedestrian.' Magazines also contained tour reports, emphasising the condition of the road surfaces, and reports from correspondents and club secretaries around the country. *The Cycling Mercury* of the 1 March 1882, for example, tells us that the John o' Groats Bicycle Club has forty members and expects that 'the Caithness roads, which are always good after March, will be in excellent condition very early this year in consequence of the absence of frost'.

Cycle Sport and Social Class

The Victorians led the world in organising and 'rationalising' athletic sports, and the high bicycle soon attracted a heavy panoply of racing rules, recording officials and argumentative governing bodies. Cycle sport was riven by codified class distinctions, and by the related amateur—professional question. The nature of the phenomenon is well illustrated by the early history of athletics. Eighteenth century pedestrianism had been an eccentric, uncodified, corrupt, gladiatorial and often savage amusement for the 'lower orders'. It was closely associated with gambling, alcohol and a casual professionalism. Events were sometimes bizarre: trundling barrow-loads of bricks, walking backwards, racing in weighted clogs, thin men carrying fat men on their backs.[8] When the upper-middle classes wanted to take up the competitive cultivation of the physique they invented a refined, respectable and strictly amateur alternative to pedestrianism, and called it athletics. This 'rationalisation' of sports, emanating principally from the universities and public schools, has become known as the 'New Athleticism'. The Amateur Athletics Club was founded in 1866 and its rules specifically barred not only professionals but even amateurs who happened to be 'mechanics, artisans and labourers'. This was also the standard policy of the Amateur Rowing Association and of the Bicycle Union, the cyclists' sporting body, set up in 1878. The Bicycle Touring Club, founded in the same year, followed the Bicycle Union in barring anyone who had ever won a prize or been paid to compete. This exclusiveness was further reflected in cricket (Gentlemen versus Players), in rugby (Union versus League) and in football (Association versus League). The rationale behind this discrimination was set out by *The Times* of the 26 April 1880:

Artisans and mechanics have, by almost general consent, been shut out from the privileged inner circle, and have been counted as in every case, professionals ... Their muscular practice is held to give them unfair advantage over more delicately nurtured competitors [and] such like troublesome persons can have no place found for them. To keep them out is a thing desirable on every account. The 'status' of the rest seems better assured and more clear from any doubt which might attach to it, and the prizes are more certain to fall into the right hands.[9]

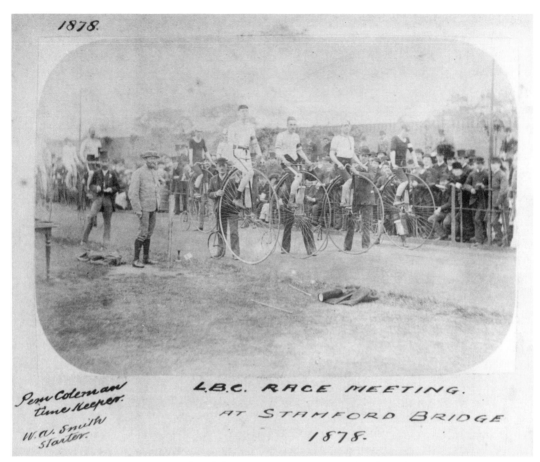

31 A London Bicycle Club race meeting at Stamford Bridge in 1878.

Organisers of amateur events kept an eye out for base mechanics or professionals who might, disguised by false whiskers and false names, plunder a few cups. And event announcements were carefully worded:

> A Two Miles' Bicycle Handicap, open to gentlemen amateurs, will be run at the Annual Athletics Sports of the Windsor and Eton Alexandra Cricket Club, which will be held in the Home Park, Windsor, on 16th September. (*The Bicycle Journal*, 8 September 1876)

Two contrasting champion riders were the Hon. Ion Keith-Falconer M.A., who became a professor of Arabic at Cambridge University in his mid-twenties, and George Waller, who was a stonemason from Newcastle upon Tyne. Keith-Falconer came from an aristocratic family in the Scottish Highlands. Having ridden a low velocipede at Harrow School he took to the high bicycle as a student at Cambridge. He was six foot, three inches tall, an exceptional height for the period, even for an aristocrat of well-nourished stock. He could master a very high machine, which gave him a competitive advantage. Keith-Falconer also had the money to buy the best bicycles and the leisure to tour extensively. Although he may have been the fastest cyclist in the world, his cycling interests were of secondary importance to him. He was also a leading theologian, linguist, propagandist of shorthand and, finally, a missionary. So amateurish was his attitude that on at least two occasions he forgot about racing engagements and turned up at short notice to win in heroic style. According to Keith-Falconer cycling served as an energetic antidote to the hours he spent on inactive bookwork. He recommended it for others as a means of character-building, since it 'keeps young fellows out of the public houses, music halls, gambling Hells and all other traps . . . As to betting, nearly all Clubs forbid it strictly, and anyone found at it is liable to be ejected promptly. A bicycle race-course is as quiet and respectable as a public science lecture by Tyndall.'[10] Despite his show of dilettantism Keith-Falconer was virtually impossible to beat. In October 1878 he raced against John Keen, the then professional champion, and beat him by five yards. Such amateur—professional matches were exceptional, however, and needed special permission.

George Waller was a different man. He was a professional rider and a Newcastle folk hero, best known for his successes in six-day endurance races. These were commercially organised indoor track events, and somewhat crasser than Keith-Falconer's rides, which were tied to the conventions of amateur athletics clubs. In April 1879 Waller put his bicycle on the train to London, to try his chances in the six-day Long Distance Championship of the World, in the Agricultural Hall, Islington. (The first such event had taken place the previous year.) Despite being the only novice among the ten competitors Waller won the championship belt and a handsome fee of 100 guineas. He returned in September to win the Championship again, riding an average of 243 miles per day. He used some of his winnings to build his own Bicycle and Recreation Ground in Newcastle. At the same time he bought a huge marquee and a detachable wooden track, about 150 yards in circumference. With these he toured the area in the company of fellow professional riders, trick cyclists, musicians and other entertainers. Waller's 'travelling circus' came to an end in Middlesbrough in 1883, when a storm destroyed the marquee. In the following year he seems to have given up his Bicycle Grounds, for reasons which are unclear, and, at the age of twenty-seven, he had returned to his first trade and was working as a jobbing builder. He died at the age of forty-five as a result of a carriage accident.[11] Keith-Falconer's calling was to missionary work in Southern Arabia, where he died of a fever at the age of thirty-two.

32 George Waller, the professional cyclist and twice winner of the six-day Long Distance Championship of the World in 1879. His championship belt, which was valued at a hundred pounds, resembles a professional boxing champion's. His machine is a fifty-three inch D.H.F. (Double Hollow Forks) Premier by Hillman, Herbert and Cooper, to whom he was professionally contracted.

33 The Hon. Ion Keith-Falconer, a gentleman amateur who was thought to be the fastest cyclist in the world in the late 1870s. His cycling interests were less important to him than his academic and missionary work.

Waller's main rival in the 1879 six-day races was Charles Terront of France. In his *Mémoires* Terront gives a vivid description of such events. He arrived late at the 1878 six-day race and found that his rivals had already put fifty miles behind them. He also found that the English riders were supplied in the saddle with food, whereas he himself had to dismount at mealtimes and rush into a nearby café. The track was unbanked and tight, which caused him nausea and vomiting. Terront's accounts of professional races in England, as well as in France, reveal precious little comradeship amongst sportsmen. He once suspected English competitors of doping his food and would accept no food offered by strangers. He also claims to have been presented with a rose laced with a stupefying drug. Yet the six-day was principally an entertainment: spectators were diverted by additions to the programme, such as the bicycle gymnastics performed in the track enclosure of the Agricultural Hall by Terront's brother.

64

The entertainment offered by men such as Waller and Terront involved unrestrained determination and physical exhaustion. At the end of his September 1879 race Waller had to be helped down from the saddle and supported on the ground. Gentleman riders, however, preferred to avoid such indignities. After prodigious cycling feats they often went walking or shooting, to reassure the world that they had not done themselves any harm. This may have been related to a belief among some members of genteel society that excessive bicycle riding could permanently damage a rider's health, and some perused the newspaper obituary columns to find cases of premature death among bicyclists.

Cycle racing, mostly on outdoor tracks, became a major national sport in the 1880s. Meetings could attract over 10,000 spectators. Whatever the triumphs of the human spirit at such events, their life-blood was the passage of money: between spectators, promoters, book-keepers, riders and sponsoring manufacturers. By the 1890s cycling was giving way to football as a major spectator sport.

The British Bicycle Industry and the Export of Enthusiasm

The British enthusiasm for bicycles brought excellent business to the manufacturers of the Midlands. Those who had entered the cycle trade in the late 1860s were joined by many others as the high bicycle became popular. Most were craftsmen who had acquired their skills in the sewing machine industry or in other related trades. Thomas Warwick and Sons, umbrella makers, began making bicycles in 1878, and the Coventry watch-making firm of Settle and Co. began in 1880. In Nottingham the engineers and machinists of the lace-making industry were attracted to bicycle manufacturing. Very few entrepreneurs had any formal training in science or technology. These mechanically minded men brought forth a constant supply of improvements and inventions. There was ambition and some insecurity, as employees broke with employers to set up their own businesses. The Coventry Machinists' Company lost James Starley, their foreman, and William Hillman, who immediately and jointly patented their Ariel bicycle, in 1870. This early machine was highly significant, being the first British all-metal high bicycle to be produced in quantity. It was sold at a reasonably accessible £8.

The success of the Ariel lay largely in the design of its front wheel. The wheel was, in a sense, the heart of the high bicycle and advances in wheel technology greatly affected the bicycle's performance and durability. The wooden velocipede wheels of the 1860s had, like cart wheels, been based on the compression principle. The uncomfortably rigid spokes were held in a wooden rim compressed by a hoop of iron which had been heated, positioned on the rim and allowed to contract as it cooled. The wire-spoked wheels of the Ariel, and of some other makes of the time, were based not on compression but on suspension: the downward force of the rider's weight was held in suspension by tensioned spokes. Such wheels were lighter and could better absorb road shocks. The Ariel's wheel had two levers which could be used to tension the spokes—all of them at once. In 1871 W. Grout introduced his own suspension wheel, in which each spoke could be tensioned individually. But in 1874 Starley introduced a design which decisively distanced the bicycle wheel from the cart wheel: he invented tangent spoking. This new method was based on the suspension principle but braced the wheel so that the driving force was more efficiently transferred from the hub to the rim. This was achieved by sending the spokes off towards the rim at an angle, adjacent spokes in almost opposite directions, so that a tangent on one side of the wheel was balanced by a tangent on the other. Tangentially arranged spokes cross each other, radially arranged spokes (as in cart wheels) do not. The standard modern bicycle wheel is tangentially spoked, and some modern racing cycles have radial spoking, usually on the front wheel only.

Ball-bearings were extensively used in British hubs from 1877 onwards, and introduced to the French, who seemed to have forgotten that they themselves had perfected and begun to use ball-bearings before their 1870 war with Prussia. In 1879 Dan Rudge, a bicycle manufacturer, walked into Charles Terront's London hotel and sold him a pair of ball-bearinged hubs. On returning to France Terront was advised by leading bicycle makers that the bearings would slow him down. He persisted in having them fitted and improved his performance times by twelve per cent.[12]

Along with the manufacture of bicycles came a wondrous supply of accessories. Bye-law obligations to make a mechanical warning noise were met by various kinds of bell. The 'American Chimes' and the 'Immaculate Alarum' dangled freely and resounded continuously like cow bells. Others could be silenced as required. The greatest din was made by the 'Arab Alarum' which was activated by the spokes of the revolving wheel at an average rate of 15,000 strokes a minute. There were also pingers, whistles, bugles and horns. Lamps were oil-fuelled. There was the 'Albion', which was 'constructed so as not to blow out in the wind', the 'Salsbury Noiseless Lamp', the 'Perfected Guiding Star' and Lucas's very successful 'King of the Road'.[13] The obligation to show a light after dark was a great imposition. Lamps were difficult to keep lit, and when it rained both the wick, and the lucifers to light it, could get wet. The problem of braking was addressed by 'Carter's Trailing Brake' which involved an iron stud dropping to the ground behind the rear wheel. It was not popular since it made the rear wheel lift. Another commercial failure, designed to alleviate the danger from

66

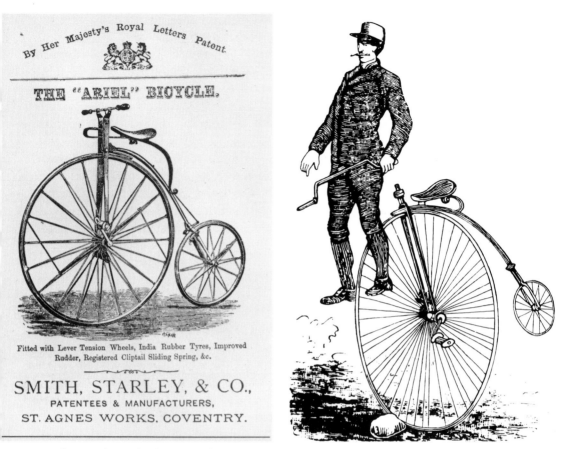

By Her Majesty's Royal Letters Patent.

THE "ARIEL" BICYCLE.

Fitted with Lever Tension Wheels, India Rubber Tyres, Improved
Rudder, Registered Cliptail Sliding Spring, &c.

SMITH, STARLEY, & CO.,
PATENTEES & MANUFACTURERS,
ST. AGNES WORKS, COVENTRY.

34 The Ariel was the first British all-metal high bicycle to be produced in quantity.
The levers connecting the hub to the wheel rim were used to tension the spokes, all
of them at once.

35 Schröter's Self-Detaching Handlebar. A German version of a doubtful idea
patented in several countries. The intention was to prevent the falling rider's legs
being pinned beneath the handlebar.

croppers, was the safety handlebar which detached from the machine at the
same time as the falling rider. There was also Jones and Reading's 'Stone
Remover' of 1885, which projected on a bracket forward of the front wheel
and flicked obstructions out of the way.

British manufacturers' exporting efforts were helped greatly by expatri-
ates who founded clubs abroad. In the Netherlands, for example, C. H.
Bingham was captain of the Ooivaar (Stork) Cycling Club of The Hague,
and D. Webster was captain of the Haarlem Cycling Club. Both being CTC
members, they initiated a similar national club for Dutch Wheelmen: the
Netherlands Cycling Federation (1883). The Berlin Bicycle Club was

founded by T. H. Walker, despite the ban on riding within the city. He popularised the bicycles of the Howe Machine Company of Glasgow, for whom he was the Berlin agent. Walker was also the editor of *Das Velociped*, Germany's first cycling periodical. Very few German nationals rode. In 1881 the Leipzig Bicycle Club consisted of four Americans, two Britons, two Italians and one German.

There were only five or so cyclists in Moscow in 1881, yet the police banned riding in the city. However, in 1883, the Howe Company were sending shipments of cycles to Moscow and in August of that year there was a bicycle racing event before a reported 30,000 spectators. One of the competitors had an immediate audience with the Governor, Prince Dolgornoff, with the result that the street-riding restrictions were lifted.[14]

In France the popular taste for cycling did not revive till the latter half of the 1880s, although the roads were relatively good and imports, principally from the Rudge Company, were available. However, the entrepreneurial challenge was taken up by Adolphe Clément in 1878, and Peugeot, makers of wire cages for crinoline dresses, began making bicycles in 1882.

The *Vélocipède Illustré*'s fictional 'Napoleon of Velocipedes' found a real-life equivalent in Colonel Albert A. Pope, the American entrepreneur and spiritual father of high-wheeling in that country. After service in the Civil War he built up the general-purpose Pope Manufacturing Company. In 1877 he began importing Singer bicycles from Coventry and in 1878 he contracted the Weed Sewing Machine Company of Hartford, Connecticut, to manufacture his Columbia bicycle, meanwhile converting part of his own factory for bicycle production. Pope was besieged by patent holders and bought up all relevant ones, including the original Lallement patent. He engaged a team of lawyers to protect his new rights and to supervise the levying of ten dollar royalties from other makers and importers.

Pope was now in a position to monopolise an American bicycle market which he had yet to create, and the crucial Lallement patent was valid for five years only. His task was not easy, for the public remembered with cynicism the undignified excesses and collapse of the velocipede craze of just ten years before. Pope hired Will Pitman, a former velocipede riding champion, who demonstrated the Columbia on the roads and public squares of New York, and was arrested for causing a disturbance. The ensuing press coverage, mostly in defence of Pitman, advertised the Columbia fulsomely. 'Some advertising is better than others,' said Pope on a different occasion, 'but all advertising is good.'[15] Pope played a leading part in the foundation, in 1878, of the Boston Bicycle Club, thought to be the first in America. The foundation of further clubs, mostly in the Boston area, was helped by a model constitution included in *The American Bicycler*, written by Charles Pratt, one of Pope's lawyers. The measured and authoritative tone of this 1880 manual dignified the public image of bicycling, and Pope paid for the distribution of many hundreds of copies to libraries and newspaper offices. He similarly circulated free copies of foreign cycling publications, which he imported himself. In 1882 Pope founded *The Wheelman*, a magazine for which he hired the talented S. S. McClure as editor. Half of each print run was distributed gratis. Pope offered prizes to doctors who published the best articles in support of cycling, and he financed law suits against municipal ordinances which were unfavourable to bicyclists. He played a major part in the foundation of the national League of American Wheelmen in 1880, which campaigned energetically for better roads. In the 1890s Pope himself was to subsidise a course in road construction at the Massachusetts Institute of Technology, and, at personal expense, he had a piece of macadam built on Columbus Avenue, Boston, to show what good roads could be like. Pope's hard work in the cause of cycling certainly prospered his business. Yet he appears to have believed firmly in the rightness of his cause and in securing benefits for the public as a whole. He was himself a touring cyclist.[16]

Pope's bicycles, and those of later competitors, were manufactured in quantity and on the principle of interchangeability of parts. This move away from individualised handworking was based on machine tool standardisation and micrometer-measuring. Pope's marketing was also standardised. His 4000 agencies sold the Columbia at a fixed price, avoiding the complex-

36 The assembly room of a bicycle factory in the US. American factories produced in quantity and on the principle of interchangeability of parts.

37 Colonel Pope's advertising sought to associate bicycle riding with elegance and respectability. This advertisement is misleading in that, with one possible exception, none of the illustrious performances cited were achieved on Columbia bicycles.

ity of price differentials in the British trade. His products fought off competition from imported British cycles, which had a reputation for superior quality but which were subject to the royalty levy and importing costs, such that their retail cost was doubled by the time they arrived.

American club riding was a particularly effective advertisement for bicycling. Regular crowds of at least 2000 watched the Boston Bicycle Club set off on its runs, and many clubs performed military-style drills and gyrations at parades and exhibitions. The major clubs had palatial headquarters. That of the Massachusetts Bicycle Club of Boston, which had 243 members in 1885, was built with financial help from Colonel Pope. It was a four-storeyed building with a ramp at the front so that cyclists could come and go without dismounting. According to an envious account in a Dutch magazine,[17] the headquarters of the New York Athletics and Velocipede Club had billiards, fencing, gymnastics and conversation rooms, and a reception room furnished in the style of Louis XIV. There were bowling alleys, a shooting range, a restaurant and a storage room for hundreds of bicycles. It had a swimming hall of Italian marble, with a pool 'as big as the opera'. The building had electric clocks, lights and waiter bells, an electro-hydraulic lift and a steam heating system. Such clubs were primarily social centres for the wealthy. It is unlikely that members would regularly face the realities of cycling on the usually dire open roads. Clubs formed by dedicated cyclists could get by without a clubhouse, and simply disbanded when roads became too rough towards winter-time. At least one club tried to train its members in rough road riding. In 1882 a visitor to Washington was invited to ride with the Capital Bicycle Club:

> There were about 45 of us, with Captain Owens at the head, and they went out for what they call practice riding, across fields and over large holes. We went over one little bank, and out of the 45 there were only seven of us got down it, all the rest went head first. I thought that was good for the machines. We all got to another place, and there was not one of us got over this. I was the fifth that went over, and I thought, 'Well, there is nothing clever in this.'[18]

The Washington club's private antics transformed into public decorum when they and other clubs took part in the League of American Wheelmen's parade to the White House, when balconies and windows held 'bouquets of pretty faces whose owners fluttered the favourite colours of the various clubs'. President Chester A. Arthur and his cabinet saluted each club from the White House steps as the 'noble six hundred' rode past, before setting off towards the Capitol to impress the senators there.[19]

It was by being ridden down the stone steps before the Capitol that, on another occasion, the American Star Bicycle demonstrated its immunity from headers. Introduced in 1881, the Star looked like a back-to-front high bicycle. The rider sat above a large lever-driven rear wheel and steered the small front wheel. The Facile and the Xtraordinary, both brought out in 1878, were British attempts to 'design away' the header problem. Their use of foot-levers enabled the rider to be seated further back, thus keeping more of his weight over the rear wheel. About the same time Rousseau of

38 The Kangaroo was a 'safety' bicycle. The gearing-up by means of chain transmission from large cog to small cog meant that a smaller front wheel could be used. Once manufacturers began applying such chain transmission to the rear wheel the era of the high bicycle began to close.

39 The Crypto-Bantam, introduced in 1893, was intended to appeal to older cyclists who could not come to terms with low, rear-wheel-driven safeties. It had a gearing-up mechanism within the front wheel hub.

40 The Star safety bicycle being ridden down the steps of the Capitol in Washington D.C.: one of the most successful publicity stunts ever.

Marseilles brought out a machine which had normal cranks attached to chainwheels which were positioned on fork extensions. On each side a chain ran up to a smaller sprocket at the wheel hub. In this way the machine was 'geared up' so as to allow the use of a smaller front wheel. A similar bicycle, the Kangaroo, was marketed by Hillman, Herbert and Cooper of Coventry from 1884. Despite its additional weight, friction and maintenance requirements it enjoyed a few years of success before being superseded by a new generation of bicycles with chain-drive to the rear wheel. High bicycles modified to lessen danger were known as 'safeties'. But the term was applied generically to all the new, low, chain-to-rear-wheel machines which were to dominate cycling from the late 1880s onwards.

The general accessibility and popularity of low, chain safeties was to seriously weaken the traditions and conventions built up by the clubmen in the course of two decades. But their innocent spirit of adventure, and their sense of participation in a new and dynamic way of life, were passed on untainted to the new cyclists of the 1890s.

73

41 Sir Arthur Conan Doyle and his wife, here outside their South Norwood home, were keen tricyclists. According to Conan Doyle it was whilst out riding that he thought up many of his ideas for stories. He endowed Sherlock Holmes with the ability to differentiate between forty-two different impressions left by cycle tyres.

4
A TENDENCY TO TRICYCLE

ATTEMPTS TO MAKE the high bicycle safer by modifying it had only limited success. It remained a cul-de-sac in terms of general design, and safety features had little effect on the bicycle's uncouth image. Yet, around 1876, some six years after the rise of the Great Wheel, manufacturers began to apply bicycle technology to the development of tricycles. The major design and marketing initiatives were taken in Britain and tricycling remained a principally British activity. Once it became clear that the new tricycles were not a resuscitation of the iron leviathans of the amateur mechanics they became popular amongst those who had been kept from the pleasures of cycling by the extremes of high-wheel bicycle design. Tricycles offered a more refined, reputable and supposedly safer alternative.

Tricycles had been ridden, to a limited extent, in the 1860s and a sense of dignity and apartness among tricyclists was becoming evident at the end of that decade:

> To the artizan or trader, or even to professional men, who leave suburban houses early in the morning, the tricycle will no doubt recommend itself, in preference to its swifter brother. It enables them to carry considerably more luggage, and also if they think fit, they may, on a wet day, avail themselves of an umbrella ... To the commercial traveller or the tourist, the tricycle will prove itself invaluable, as ... they can stop when and where they please, without perilling their limbs by jumping off. The tourist may balance the steering handle, and rest to enjoy a fine prospect, or he may eat his bread and drink his wine under the shade of the nearest tree, with no ghost of equilibrium to make him afraid.[1]

Tricycling was taken up by older, less athletic members of the respectable professions, and was favoured by clergymen and doctors. It was espoused by members of the upper classes as a dignified form of recreation. Although the relationship between tricyclists and bicyclists seems to have been quite amicable on the roads some cyclists came to associate their sense of class allegiance with the number of wheels one chose to ride on. In priggish letters to the cycling press tricyclists sought to distance themselves from bicycling *hoi polloi* and claimed that their status and more mature behaviour should entitle them to exemption from anti-cycling legislation such as riding bans in the London parks. The bye-laws resulting from the 1878 Highways and Locomotives (Amendment) Act concerned themselves with bicycles specifically and left tricycles outside the legislative net. Few bicyclists considered this to be a mere oversight on the part of the law-makers. There was even some doubt about the administration of the Common Law. A *Cyclist* editorial of the 11 February 1882 claimed that 'County Court judges seem to look more favourably on tricycles than they do on bicycles.' In 1882 or 1883 a circular was sent to tricycling members of the Bicycle Touring Club:

> It is desired by most Tricyclists to separate themselves entirely from the Bicyclists, who are a disgrace to the pastime, while Tricycling includes Princes, Princesses, Dukes, Earls etc. There are none of the upper circle who ride Bicycles. This is easily seen, and it is plain that the Tricyclists are altogether a better class than the Bicyclists, and require better accommodation on tours, etc. A new Tricycling Union has been formed, and could not that body make itself a Tricycle Touring Club as well?[2]

The circular also contained some advice for recipients: 'Please do not show this to your [BTC] Consul unless he is sure to join us.' A Tricycle Association had already been formed, in late 1880, but had amalgamated with the Bicycle Union in February 1882. A break-away Tricycle Union was founded in December 1882, but was never really successful and, after two years, became the Society of Cyclists, following 'the higher aims of cycling'. It did not thrive.

One basic reason for the tricycle's role as a denominator of class was its expense. The mechanical complexity of tricycles made them two or even three times as expensive as a bicycle of comparable quality. It is possible that costs were increased by the shortness of production runs: the huge potential for design changes, which was so lacking in two-wheeler technology, encouraged rapid obsolescence and could leave manufacturers with expensive but unsellable stock on their hands. Those consumers who saw their tricycles as tokens of their status would want to be seen riding (and affording) the latest models.

The sheer size of tricycles tended to restrict ownership to those classes who had a stable or outhouse at home, although some machines, such as Starley and Sutton's 'Compressus', were designed to fold into a narrower width. *The Tricyclist*, a periodical founded in 1882, urged the establishment of 'town stables for tricycles', so that men riding in to their London clubs and offices might park their bulky vehicles in a safe and central place. An editorial of the 19 January 1883 envisaged that such a store might offer standing space for an annual two or three pounds and employ 'handy lads to clean and look after machines'. It would thus encourage 'town parties' of tricyclists who would join together each morning to ride in from the suburbs.

Owners of large-wheeled Sociables, which allowed two riders to sit side by side, had even greater storage problems, and were particularly penalised when they put such a massive machine on the railways. The railway companies had to lay on an open 'carriage truck' of the kind used to transport town families' horse and carriages to seaside resorts for the season. In one case a Sociable owner was charged seventeen shillings carriage, whereas a lesser machine would have gone in the guard's van for two shillings.[3] The bulk of tricycles was sometimes an asset. According to an advance announcement of the League of American Wheelmen's Washington Meet in 1884, there was to be 'a strong body of tricyclers ... as flankers to keep the crowd back to the sidewalk'.[4]

Cycling club photographs show that an increasing number of members were turning to tricycles, although they will have needed to be superior athletes to keep up with their two-wheeled associates on club runs. Some clubs bought a tandem tricycle or a Sociable for the use of individual members, many of whom will have used their 'club bus' for courting

42 'Sociable' riding in the cool of the evening in 1886 on Riverside Drive, one of the few roads in New York City with a surface friendly to cyclists. Tricycling did not become widely popular in the United States.

purposes. The sadly extinct Sociable was unique in that it allowed partners to ride along arm in arm. Separate tricycle clubs were formed, mainly in the big cities. The important London Tricycle Club excluded women, but female membership was welcomed by many other clubs, such as the South London Tricycle Club, whose secretary reported a memorable outing:

> Twelve members on eight singles and two Sociables to Sydenham ... On the return journey the crank of a Sociable snapped just as the party reached Dulwich Station. By pushing the machine up-hill, riding it down, and taking it in tow by the other Sociable on the level, Brixton was safely reached at 10.30, whence the lady-riders went home by train.[5]

Before the advent of the tricycle very few women had managed to cycle without attracting criticism. The rare references we have to female high bicycle riders suggest they were employed as public entertainers: in the Folies Bergères, for example. An American lady, Mrs Reginald de Koven, recalled in 1895 that some women 'lost all sense of feminine discretion' and rode the high wheel 'in the days when it was in common use at athletic shows, dime museums, circuses and such like unholy places'. The same indignant lady had taken to tricycle riding as a teenager and considered it a liberating experience, especially for younger women. Many of her sex, she said, 'remembered the wild excitement of riding a red-wheeled tricycle, borrowed from a reluctant brother or friend, as one of the ... joys of childhood'.[6] There was, in the late nineteenth century, an increasing upper middle-class interest in sporting activities which men and women could enjoy together, such as golf, croquet, archery and tennis. Tricycling offered a further opportunity. The customary and convenient male view that women should be lovingly protected from over-exertion was weakening in the 1880s, and by 1885 women tricyclists were generally accepted. However, sensitive ladies of rank were still liable to be offended by roadside comments from the lower orders. In the United States, where tricycling was distinctly uncommon, women founded their own tricycling clubs for common protection, and would-be female tricyclists were advised to avoid the critical public in New York's Central Park, but rather to take the train to East Orange, New Jersey, where there were quiet roads to practice on.[7]

There was inevitable discussion as to the most appropriate tricycling wear for women. *The Cyclist* of the 26 April 1882 reported that some lady club tricyclists were wearing a male-style uniform, but with a 'wirey serge skirt which does not cling to the body ... Ladies can, of course, use a great deal of coloured braid in a costume without it looking outré.' On the 24 August 1881 *The Cyclist* reported a remarkable garment intended for 'the gentler members of the tricycular ranks'. It was the 'Velocipedienne', patented by Messrs Samuel Brothers, outfitters, and consisted of

43 Touring tricyclists at St Andrews, East Fife, in about 1890, after having ridden from Edinburgh. They are John Puckering J.P., his daughter, Rose, and his wife, Emma. They are riding Quadrant tricycles. Quadrants were first made in 1882 and became very popular thanks to their unwillingness to tip forwards or backwards and their positive steering. The front wheel was made to turn by the axle sliding along slots in the forks. Front-, as opposed to rear-wheel steering, was in itself a great advance, as rear steering wheels could lose their grip on the road. The Quadrant's larger front wheel also helped.

a cleverly constructed arrangement of cords and pulleys, attached to and concealed in the skirt, which, whilst not detracting in any way from its usefulness as a dress for ordinary wear, instantly adapts itself to the peculiar exigencies of tricycle riding when necessary, for by drawing a cord the fulness of the skirt in the rear is drawn in out of the way of the chains and wheels, whilst at the same time the feet and ankles are hidden from the vulgar gaze by a neat fold.

Stability was the great advantage of tricycles. Unlike bicycles they could go at very low speeds without keeling over, and there was no need to get off and on again at every hold-up in the traffic. Stability at minimal speeds helped sufficiently low-geared tricycles to get up hills, and tricyclists often beat bicyclists in hill-climbing competitions, despite their extra weight and friction. However, an averagely geared touring tricycle, loaded up with all the luggage a bicyclist could never accommodate, would be beaten by quite gentle hills, and the *CTC Gazette* of May 1884 carried some appropriate advice from a reader:

> When touring in a hilly country, it is better to fasten a rope, about four yards long, to the ends of the foot-rest, and *draw* the machine up unrideable hills instead of *pushing* it, as the rope goes round the waist and the arms get a rest ... I have pulled my 'Humber' up the Brünig Pass, in Switzerland, for 1½ hours without fatigue.

The bicyclist had a single-track machine, but the tricyclist usually made three tracks. The former could choose any part of the roadway, even the smooth base of a waggon rut; the latter preferred the crown of the road so as to avoid a sideways lean, but had to aim for a part of the road which suited each of her three wheels. Some lurching about on rough roads was inevitable. It was not clear whether tricycles were any safer than bicycles. Any of

44 Since the early days of human-powered vehicles tricycles have given invalids mobility. There's a strong sense of pride and independence in this studio photograph from Gateshead, Tyneside. The long tradition of manumotive tricycles is still maintained in the Third World and to some degree in the Netherlands.

45 The Coventry Rotary was the first widely popular tricycle. It was steered by means of the spade grip handle and both small wheels were linked together so as to turn in unison.

the three wheels might hit a stone or hole, causing the machine to tip over. And, as tricyclists sat in their vehicles rather than on them, they could not easily leap clear before an accident and were not easily thrown clear in the course of one, being more likely to be entangled in their cartwheeling machinery. Any loss of control on a hill with a bend in it could prove fatal, and desperate attempts to re-engage feet on whirring pedals could themselves lead to entanglement. Tricycles were only safe if conservatively ridden. Some doctors used them for night call-outs since they could be ridden slowly over potholes hidden in the dark. They also obviated the need to make a horse ready in the middle of the night, and could carry a sizeable doctor's bag.

The tricycles of the 1860s had been mostly standard velocipedes fitted with a free-running two-wheel rear axle. Tricycle technology in the 1870s was dominated and developed by the inventiveness of James Starley. Starley's first production tricycle, the Coventry Lever Tricycle, evolved from a failed bicycle project. In 1874 he had patented a version of the Ariel high bicycle which was intended to be ridden by women with long skirts. The backbone and rear wheel were offset and the lady was expected to sit with both legs to one side of the front wheel, both treadles being positioned on that one side. Starley made the best of this uncharacteristically bad job by adding an extra wheel for stability and by improving the steering, drive and seating arrangements. The result was the Coventry Lever Tricycle, which was first marketed in 1877 and was a great success. When the lever-drive was replaced by chain-drive it was renamed the Coventry Rotary Tricycle and, later, the Rudge Rotary. Starley's next major tricycle project was the Salvo-Quadricycle—a tricycle despite its name since the fourth wheel was no more than a raised safety wheel which extended forwards (and later, backwards) on an arm, so as to prevent the machine from tipping. Such wheels were to become common on tricycles. The Salvo had other significant design features: continuous chain drive, a lever-operated hand brake and a 'balance gear', later to be known as a differential. The balance gear enabled power to be transmitted equally to both wheels and yet allowed one wheel to follow its natural propensity to rotate faster than the other when the machine was cornering. The Salvo was a great success and agents were appointed throughout the country. A daughter of an agent in the Isle of Wight happened to be riding a Salvo within eyeshot of Queen Victoria, who was passing in her carriage. The monarch was much taken by the machine and ordered two of them. Starley was received by Queen Victoria when he delivered one of them in 1881, and the Salvo was renamed the 'Royal Salvo', although Queen Victoria is unlikely to have ever ridden her acquisitions. Starley died of cancer later in the same year and was greatly missed. His gifts as a problem-solving mechanic and inspired inventor had been matched by his integrity and unassuming good nature. A good biography of the man has yet to be written.

In the year of Starley's death a Coventry trade gazette reported that the tricycle trade in that city had become better than the bicycle trade.[8] At each of the Stanley (Cycle) Shows from 1883 to 1886 there were more tricycles exhibited than bicycles. By this period almost all major manufacturers had at least one model of tricycle in their catalogues and they copiously supported their products with glowing testimonials from people of position in society. The standard practice was for firms to write to past customers asking how pleased they were with their purchase. Unflattering replies could be put to one side and favourable responses published.

Many of the principal tricycle designs were imitated abroad: by Clément in France, Kleyer in Germany and Overman in the United States. However, the desirability of British-made machines maintained a good flow of exports, helped along by some prestigious sales coups. The Royal Court of Austro-Hungary ordered five Cheylesmores from the Coventry Machinists' Company, having perhaps been encouraged by the fact that the Prince

46 Riders of Salvo-Quadricycles at Old Steine, Brighton, in the late 1870s, wearing a fine variety of hats. Their machines' inventor, James Starley, dubbed the Father of the Cycle Industry, is almost certainly the darkly dressed gentleman in the centre. On early versions the Salvo-Quadricycle's safety wheel was at the front and the steering wheel at the back. The arrangement was reversed on later models.

47 The Folkestone Cycling Club in about 1885: a mixture of tricycles, tandem tricycles, geared-up safety high bicycles, and one lever-driven Singer Xtraordinary safety high bicycle (back row, second from right). There appears to be not one standard non-safety high bicycle.

of Wales had ordered one. The indigenous potentates of colonised lands provided another market. In 1882, for example, Rudge and Co. supplied a tricycle to Solhikoff, H. H. The Moharana Sahib Bahadur of Oodypore. Such machines were intended to be propelled by servants rather than owners. In Germany there was a particular interest in the replacement of horse cabs by human powered vehicles. In 1885 the Hamburg firm of Lenning brought out the five-wheeled Fugitive, which had provision for five riders plus standing room for a non-pedalling guest. Dumstrey and Jungck of Berlin produced the Sultan Cycle Carriage, which was a form of rickshaw quadricycle for two passengers and two pedallers.[9]

Tradesmen began to look at the potential of tricycles for more mundane purposes, and such goods as groceries and newspapers were carried, although the heyday of the carrier cycle lay yet in the future. In Britain and

48 The Coventry Machinists' Co.'s Coolie-Cycle was exported, in single and double versions, to the sultans and rajahs of the Empire. The use of Europeans in the drawing was probably meant to suggest the machine's prestige value as a facet of Western civilisation.

49 The tandem tricycle was a very efficient vehicle since the efforts of two riders were applied to a machine which was little heavier than a solo. Models such as this Humber were, however, very difficult to control at speed. They offered less wind resistance than the side-by-side Sociables which they came to supersede. The riders here are Scheltema-Beduin of the Trekvogels Club, Amsterdam, and Basil Crump of the London Bicycle Club. Together they set up a (paced) hour record of 20 miles 95 yards in 1890.

84

50 The Post Office ordered its first carrier tricycles in 1881 and the results were satisfactory. However, the Horsham depot experimented with this locally built pentacycle, familiarly known as the 'Hen and Chickens'. It did not meet with success, partly because the large drive-wheel sometimes dipped into a hole in the road but was prevented by the support wheels from getting traction.

Germany at least, milk was delivered by tricycle in the 1880s and dispensed from large churns. There was also the Photographic Tricycle: a Coventry Rotary equipped with a large box camera which could be swivelled on a pedestal rising from the centre of the frame. It had storage boxes for photographic plates and other materials. Again, there was the Huntsman's Tricycle, produced by Seidel and Neumann of Dresden, which was designed to carry the rider's guns and hunting gear.

Perhaps the most imaginative machine was the amphibious tricycle built by William Terry, a twenty-nine year old nautical man. In 1883 he rode it from London to Dover, converted it into a rowing boat and crossed the Channel. On arriving in France he was detained for a while on suspicion of smuggling. Once he was released the local cycling club organised a public demonstration of his invention on a canal, after which Mr Terry cycled by land to Paris. His machine resembled a normal tricycle. The two large wheels were made in two equal parts joined together by bolts. The four half-wheels formed (somehow) the hull of the boat, and the tricycle's backbone divided up so as to provide struts for internal support. The only components which did not have a function on the tricycle were a long piece of wood, which braced the hull and acted as a keel, and two twenty-litre air bags attached either side. The cycling press described his feat with reverence, for tricycles were dignified machines and were regarded as promising vehicles for the application of imagination and ingenuity.[10]

5
THE TRIUMPH OF SAFETY-CYCLING

The Early Days of Safety Cycling

THE DECISIVE ARRIVAL and development of the low, rear-wheel-driven safety bicycle, between about 1885 and 1891, sent the high-wheel bicycle into irreversible decline. It caused defections among tricyclists and attracted many new converts. To distinguish them from the newcomers, high bicycles became additionally known as Ordinaries.

In the course of 1884 several British manufacturers brought out low

51 An 1885 version of the Rover safety bicycle which 'set the fashion to the world'. The early Rovers were mounted by means of a foot-step on the rear of the frame, as had been the case with high bicycles. This was a sensible arrangement in the days before the freewheel mechanism. Once in the saddle the rider could catch up with the revolving pedals. Another inheritance from the high bicycle tradition was the upright sitting position. A further Rover model, with curves on all main tubes, was brought out later in 1885.

86

52 After a 'meet' of London cycling clubs at Woodford in 1888, the clubmen rode home in a Chinese lantern procession. This evocative sketch from the *Illustrated London News* shows that the high bicycle was losing its monopoly amongst clubmen.

bicycles, but it was the 1885 Rover, designed by John Kemp Starley, nephew of James Starley, which 'set the fashion to the world'. It became internationally identified with the design type as a whole (such that the modern Polish word for 'bicycle' is *rower*). The speed and safety of the new Rovers were publicised by the Rover Road Race in September 1885, organised by the manufacturers, Starley and Sutton, who themselves awarded all prizes. They had advertised a false venue so as to hoodwink the police, who were liable to suppress road events.

The Rover front wheel was slightly larger than the rear, giving more positive steering and better cushioning than the small front wheels of rival safeties. The Rover improved on the high bicycle by being adjustable to suit riders of varying physiques. Handlebar and seat positions could be altered and, importantly, it had a changeable chainwheel and rear sprocket, which allowed for alterations to the gearing. Many high-wheel riders failed to take the squat new safeties seriously, looking down upon them both physically and figuratively. They had already seen off one premature version, Lawson's 1879 Bicyclette, condemned as ugly and called the 'Crocodile'. The

87

2381. Sogn, Nærødalen, Velocipeder.   Axel Lindahl.

53 Cyclists on solid-tyred machines in Norway, probably in the early 1890s. Not only were safety bicycles more manageable on difficult terrain, but they could carry much more luggage than the high bicycle. These tourists are riding cross-frame machines, a short-lived but popular alternative to the stronger open-diamond Rover design. The figures on the left remain upright by holding each other's handlebars.

post-1884 machines met with nicknames such as 'beetle' and 'crawler'. They were dismissively associated with older people, women, and those of timid disposition. And were not the low safeties, with their almost equal-sized wheels, a throw-back to the days of the hobby-horse and the 1860s boneshakers? Yet the new machines performed demonstrably well and manufacturers concentrated on refining them.

At least one criticism of the low safety was valid: smaller wheels may have been safer but they tended to be uncomfortable, lacking the high wheel's ability to ride easily over holes and bumps. Sprung saddles helped, and another response to the problem was to suspend the frame within springs, as exemplified by the Whippet, which was popular around 1887. Few dared to predict future trends. In the mid-1880s the roads were enlivened by an impressive variety of cycle designs. Those wishing to join the throng could choose between traditional high bicycles, geared-up safety high bicycles such as the Kangaroo, about two hundred divergent designs of tricycle and quadricycle, and low safeties in various configurations.

In 1888, a year in which British factories turned out six times as many low safeties as high bicycles, John Boyd Dunlop patented his pneumatic bicycle tyre, a development perhaps as significant as the arrival of the low safety itself. Dunlop, a Scottish veterinary surgeon working in Belfast, came upon the idea of fitting air-filled tyres to his young son's tricycle. The innovation worked and led to commercial production.

When Dunlop's pneumatics were first ridden in competitive events their success dumbfounded spectators and unprepared race officials. Production moved from Dublin to Belfast, and then to Coventry so as to be near the heart of the trade. The early tyres were glued on and were fitted in the Dunlop factory itself. The firm's carts travelled around the city fetching wheels from cycle factories and returning them tyred. The public was fascinated by the novel tyres. When one of the first pneumatic-tyred bicycles was left outside a Coventry hotel for ten minutes it attracted, according to the rider, a crowd of four or five hundred people who jostled to see it. There was some ridicule. Popular epithets were 'bladder-wheel', 'windbag',

54 The cyclists of the 2nd Volunteer Battalion, the Gloucestershire Regiment, in 1888, the year in which such cycling corps were first allowed. Only the officer has a tricycle and owners of high bicycles are demoted to the back row. The army hoped that cycle-mounted troups would take an active fighting role but was to find that they were more useful as messengers and scouts.

'pudding-tyre' and, in Germany, 'liver sausage tyre'. Some claimed that the flattening of the tyre on contact with the road caused an effect similar to riding permanently uphill. There were rumours of pneumatics becoming dangerously hot, and of cyclists being blinded by exploding tyres. Some thought, with a degree of justification, that pneumatics were too puncture-prone. They could take up to four hours to repair. According to the notoriously reactionary Lord Randolph Churchill they had a further draw-back: he explained to the House of Commons in 1894 that pneumatic-tyred bicycles were a public danger since they 'come silently and stealthily upon one'. Despite all objections, aesthetic or otherwise, the comfort and rolling efficiency of pneumatics won through. The Dunlop Company acquired the 1890 'Welch' patent for 'wired-on' tyres, which made puncture repair much easier, and by 1892 cyclists at the leading edge of the vogue had demoted their solid-tyred bicycles to the second hand market. Few such machines had enough fork and frame clearance to permit the simple replacement of solid by pneumatic wheels. A few high bicycles were equipped with air-filled tyres but the idea did not become popular.

Dunlop's patent turned out to be worthless when it was discovered that there existed an 1845 patent for pneumatic tyres intended for horse-carriage wheels. However, competition was outpaced thanks to the enthusiasm and business acumen of Dunlop's backers, the du Cros family, and to the 'wired-on' patent. In France an easily detachable tubeless tyre was de-veloped by Edouard Michelin in 1891. Charles Terront, who had forsaken the *grand bicycle* for the low *bicyclette* in 1889, won the 1891 Paris-Brest-Paris race on Michelin's tyres, despite being held up by five punctures caused by hobnails fallen from peasants' boots. One of the repairs took the Michelin mechanic forty minutes, much to Terront's annoyance.[1] In the following year the Michelin Company organised a road race from Paris to Clermont-Ferrand with the express purpose of demonstrating the superior-ity of their tyres over Dunlop's. According to one unsupported source,[2] nails were scattered on the road at pre-arranged places, with a Michelin repair team waiting conveniently nearby. A Michelin bicycle won the race and the firm announced that its product was 'unbeatable'. The low safety bicycle and pneumatic tyres had been pioneered by competitive sportsmen, who cared more about results than the niceties of fashion. From about 1888 the new developments began to find favour with leisure cyclists, and the Local Government Act of 1888 further improved the social position of cycling. Parliament increased the cycle's legal status as a road vehicle and laid down legislation which superseded the patchwork of local by-laws which had afflicted cyclists. This was the result of confident lobbying by the CTC, helped, perhaps, by the fact that some of its more influential members were of the same social class as Members of Parliament.

The enhanced and enhancing status of cycling, and its promises of novel,

55 Charles Terront, France's first sports 'star' on his Michelin-tyred Humber after having won the 1891 Paris–Brest–Paris race. He came from a poor working-class background and began his cycling career by competing on hired wooden velocipedes. He became successful at high bicycle racing and converted well to safeties. Terront became the model for a whole generation of working-class youths who sought fame and fortune through cycle sport. His achievements in the corrupt and brutal world of professional cycling earned him, among other things, a reserved seat at the Opéra de Paris.

adventurous, liberating patterns of leisure, attracted members of the lower middle class. 'The two sections of the community which form the majority of "wheelmen"', stated *The Cyclist* of 13 August 1892, 'are the great clerk class and the great shop assistant class.' Shop assisting was then a predominantly male profession occupying an indeterminate position in the nether regions of middle-class society. Both protagonists in H. G. Wells's *History of Mr. Polly* and *Kipps* work in draper's shops and buy bicycles as an aid to social mobility. Polly's bicycle enables him to make middle-class 'visitations' on distant friends and relatives, and helps him court a woman living some way off. It also gives him sporadic surges of the spirit in the face of the drabness of shop life. A bicycle was a major investment for the lower middle classes—both of Wells's heroes bought their machines as a result of sudden legacies. Bicycle buyers might otherwise pay by instalments. Wells's major cycling novel was *The Wheels of Chance* (1896). The hero, Hoopdriver, is yet another draper's assistant, as Wells himself had been. He devotes his annual holiday to a ten-day cycle tour of the South Coast, along a route previously taken by Wells himself, who had just learned to cycle. Hoopdriver sets out one morning 'with a dignified curvature of path' and wearing his new brown cycling suit, a Norfolk jacket. His old fashioned bicycle transports him to a new world:

> Here was quiet and greenery, and one mucked about as the desire took one, without a soul to see ... Once he almost ran over something wonderful, a little, low, red beast with a yellowish tail, that went rushing across the road before him. It was the first weasel he had ever seen in his cockney life. There were miles of this, scores of miles of this before him.

His mode of transport brings him into contact with a New Woman, an

56 The Easington Lane Bicycle Club outside the Bonnie Pit Laddie public house, Easington, Durham, in about 1892. The machines in the centre are cross-frames, and the bicycle second from the left is a new up-to-date diamond frame safety. Unusual for this date, the club has a bugler (front row, second right).

independently minded young lady from the upper middle classes who was cycling unchaperoned well away from home. Hoopdriver becomes infatuated with her and rescues her from her pursuing suitor who claims that she has sullied her reputation by leaving home with him (the suitor) on a bicycle, and therefore has no option but to marry him. The shift in social perspectives, as exemplified by Wells's cyclists, led Galsworthy to claim, at a later date, that the bicycle had 'been responsible for more movement in manners and morals than anything since Charles the Second'.[3]

The great transition to safety cycling did not help the fortunes of the CTC, whose membership dropped, for no apparent external reason, from 22,316 in 1886 to 14,166 in 1894. Individual cycling clubs tended to become more urbane, informal and, in many cases, mixed-sex. Typical was the Potternewton Cycling Club, of Leeds. Although the club had its own 'racing men' and records committee, the Potternewton's hundred or so members enjoyed a substantial social life which was strengthened by a homely but expensively produced monthly magazine. There was a 'suburban headquarters' in a local hotel, and an additional city centre headquarters was established as membership grew. Each cycling club attracted members from a specific social level, a phenomenon by no means restricted to Britain. The Hull Grosvenor Cycling Club was larger than the Potternewton, and with a membership fee of 2s 6d, was less exclusive. Any admiration for the Hull club was headed off by the Potternewton's magazine editor: 'A hundred members at 7s 6d is infinitely superior to three hundred at 2s 6d. A subscription of 2s 6d is absurdly low in our mind, and almost too small to keep the club respectable.'[4]

The safety bicycle was received enthusiastically throughout Europe and in the United States, and was adapted to the cultural ethos and class structure of each country. 'The Frenchmen who go in for cycling', it was observed in 1888, 'are all of the better class, the lower orders could not afford to do it ... the French rider at present looks to England for his machine for he can afford to gratify his tastes and obtain the very best.'[5] Just a few years later, when French-made cycles were more available, it was bourgeois France which espoused the bicycle, hailing it as a symbol of the nation's enterprise and vigour, of modernity and democracy. 'Cours, vélo, cours dans ta lumière/le progrès chevauche sur toi', wrote the poet, Deckert.[6] In the previous two decades physical prowess had been promoted as a public virtue, and even as a patriotic duty. Many believed that France had lost the war of 1870 because of a deterioration in its racial stock. There was a huge increase in the number of gymnastics clubs, which, it was hoped, would raise the level of physical fitness to that of the Prussian arch-enemy.[7] Although cycling benefitted only indirectly from this fitness movement its praises were often sung in terms of revolutionary fervour or strident nationalism. In *Le Figaro* of the 4 October 1890 a literary supplement on cycling included twenty-two illustrations of Mars on a bicycle, and the French *Cyclists' Yearbook* of 1893 announced: 'Each century completes its course with a great upheaval. 1793 was marked by blood and the guillotine, 1893 by rubber and ball-bearings.'

By 1893 the French bourgeoisie were joining cycle clubs in large numbers. A big city might have a dozen clubs, each appealing to a specific social class. The élite sports clubs for amateur gentlemen remained largely unassailed, new cyclists preferring to set up clubs of their own. A small provincial town would have only one cycling club, which would draw members from a wide social spectrum. Many French cyclists liked (and still like) to assume a racy image and middle-class males wore the short jacket and tight breeches of the professional racing man. Bicycle prices were dauntingly high. A young primary school teacher working in the Normandy countryside recalled that he needed to borrow money from his father, a farmer, and his uncle, a mason, in order to buy a second hand bicycle in 1898. Even though prices had begun to fall by this date the retail cost of a bicycle would represent three months of a primary schoolteacher's pay. It took five years to repay the loans.[8]

Whereas the French state smiled kindly upon the bicycle, cyclists in Germany were met by the forces of conservatism. Wilhelm II's disdain was matched at ground level by the legislatures of individual states, provinces and cities. The touring cyclist needed to be familiar with the intricacies of cycle law in each province en route. Many roads, both rural and urban, including 50 per cent of all Bavarian roads, were closed to cyclists, or else open only between certain times of day. Most provinces insisted on single-file riding, and on busier streets cyclists were obliged to ride at distances of ten metres from each other. Tourists who failed to notice relevant road signs, or who otherwise transgressed, were at the mercy of plain clothes policemen who sometimes hid behind trees or in ditches. Most provinces required cyclists to carry a 'bicycle pass' which identified the rider, gave permission to ride, and could be withdrawn. In some states cyclists under fourteen could ride only if they carried a 'certificate of competence' issued by the police. Cyclists under eighteen needed a similar document signed by their employer or a magistrate. The freedom, mobility and privacy of the bicycle were more than the authorities would tolerate. Significantly, Germany was one of the first nations to provide bicycles for its policemen and local militias—agents of social control.

The welter of restrictions could do no more than hamper the progress of cycling in Germany. There were about half a million German cyclists in 1896 and the German Cycling Federation represented five hundred clubs in German-speaking Europe. The ethos of these clubs was one of nature-loving athleticism. There was, for example, the *Wanderlust* Club in Leipzig and the Over Mount and Vale Club in Kleve. The German enthusiasm for

57 An advertisement for the Presto Cycle works, Germany. A common theme was the escaping by bicycle from dangerous animals or African tribesmen.

cycling as a means of communing with nature could reach spiritual proportions, as evidenced in an 1890 guide to cycling by Wilhelm Wolf: 'How greatly does cycling ennoble one's spirit, heart and frame of mind! When the cyclist roams freely on his steely steed in the godly world of Nature ... his heart rises and he bewonders the splendour of Creation.'[9] Wolf's book also gives indication that cycling in Germany became embroiled in prevailing class conflicts: 'Which cyclist does not have daily experience, especially when riding through city suburbs breathed on by Social Democracy, of unruly urchins dancing about in front of his wheel, throwing sticks and stones, being foul-mouthed and more besides. And often many of the adults in these districts, standing idly at their doors on Sundays and holidays, are not averse to such behaviour.' Wolf goes on to advise on how to cope with 'the hate which coachmen and other people of the lower orders seem presently to harbour against cyclists'. The middle-class cyclists of Germany seem to have been oppressed both by state authoritarianism and working-class antagonism. It is small wonder that cycling manuals contained lengthy sections on cyclists' rights. One such book devoted seventy pages to the subject: an eighth of its contents.[10]

As cycling became more popular across Europe there arose the problem of compatibility with one's profession. Armies were forced to decide whether their officers should cycle in uniform when off duty. In 1891 the Belgian Minister of War banned the practice, but was forced to relent two years later, permitting uniformed riding in the mornings only. The Roman Catholic clergy were deterred from cycling until Pope Leo XIII had a change of heart in 1894. Competitive cycling was felt to be particularly unbecoming for a professional man. Henri Desgrange, who was later to found the Tour de France, lost his job with a law firm when his client complained that his activities as a champion sprint rider were incompatible with the dignity of the law. In 1896 a Dutch commissioner of police forbade his men to cycle, even in their free time, and yet in other parts of that country bicycles were being introduced for police work.

Once policemen were put on bicycles they could, at last, chase and apprehend errant cyclists, although the cycling world buzzed with rumours of other methods, such as a large net to be thrown over cyclists in Amsterdam. Theodore Roosevelt, who was a New York City police commissioner in the mid 1890s, recalled that his bicycling policemen 'frequently stopped runaways, wheeling alongside of them, and grasping the horses, (and) they

58 The Police Patrol Tricycle produced by the Davis Sewing Machine Company of Dayton, Ohio, in 1898. It was made for transporting offenders to the lock-up and had provision for securing them hand and foot.

59 A tram car for cyclists in Butte, Montana, in 1893. American public transport authorities were quick to offer facilities for cyclists. Regular cyclists' day excursion trains left New York City in the mid-1890s and cyclists were allowed on the elevated steam railway in Brooklyn.

managed not only to overtake, but to jump into the vehicle and capture, on two or three different occasions, men who were guilty of reckless driving, and who fought violently in resisting arrest.'[11] The New York Police also hired the speed-cycling star, Mile-a-Minute Murphy, to catch transgressing cyclists.

Bicycle manufacturing in the United States was dominated by the Pope Manufacturing Company and the Overman Wheel Company. Their rivalry was bitterly argumentative. Overman was first to bring out a low safety, the 1887 Victor, marketed a year before Pope brought out his first low safeties. Pope sold his wares with more panache. One ploy was to offer a fifty dollar reward to anyone who returned a stolen Columbia, still in good condition, to its owner—but only on conviction of the thief. 'It is grand larceny to steal a bicycle; it is arrest and conviction to steal a "Columbia"', he declared. In his 1893 catalogue Pope explained that he was the first to introduce the bicycle into the regular army and urged that his machines be used by the post office, messengers and policemen. For volunteer firemen he made available a bicycle carrying a fire extinguisher and a fireman's axe.[12]

Lightness became a prime requirement for American bicycles and was made possible by some heavy investment by manufacturers. Pope's weldless steel tubing plant was completed in 1892: cycle technology which only the English had hitherto possessed. At about the same time he set up advanced metallurgical laboratories and introduced stress-measuring gauges.

97

Wooden rims reduced weight, and bicycles were marketed with fewer accessories. Even brakes became unfashionable on men's models after about 1894, but 'scorchers' rode 'fixed-wheel' (without a freewheel mechanism) and could use back-pressure to brake. The industry expanded rapidly. In 1890 twenty-seven factories produced about 40,000 bicycles. Six years later 250 factories were producing 1,200,000 machines. Marketing was intensive, taking up about 10 per cent of all newspaper advertising in the mid 1890s. There was extensive selling through department stores and hire purchase arrangements became common.

Lightweight bicycles found an eager market among the members of the Century Riding Club of America, who were awarded a gold bar each time they rode a hundred miles on public roads within twenty-four hours (later reduced to fourteen hours as a result of over-success).

There was an increase in long distance leisure cycle-touring in the United States, supported by a complex of ancillary services. There were maps and guides, supplemented by direction and 'dangerous hill' signs erected by the League of American Wheelmen; there were repair shops and LAW-evaluated hotels; there were roadside stalls from which farmers, who were badly affected by an agricultural depression, sold their produce; and there were trains to take cyclists a little further on their tour, or back to their cities. In 1894 the railways carried 430,000 cyclists and their machines. In an article on the history of early American cycle-touring Gary A. Tobin argues that the pastime was not motivated by any anti-urban tendency: riders sought a controlled contact with nature, combined with a maximum of urban culture. The 'service corridors' along which they cycled represented a new form of urban growth. Cyclists who strayed beyond these 'corridors' risked the dangers of a hostile environment, and many carried firearms for fear of attack by robbers.[13] Sears and Roebuck marketed a collapsible 'bicycle rifle' which could be used as either a pistol or a rifle.

Most cycle-tourists were sophisticates of the Eastern Seaboard area. However, in September 1893, a great number of cyclists were among the 100,000 people waiting in squalid camps along the border of Cherokee Strip, an Indian reservation in Arkansas which was about to be declared 'open'. The bicyclists, each loaded up with a canteen of water, provisions and blankets, reckoned on staking claims to the choicest land ahead of other hopefuls on horseback. There were about thirty women among the cyclists, who all suffered great privation.[14]

It was in the arid Western Australian Bush, and particularly during the goldrushes of 1892 to about 1897, that the bicycle consistently showed its usefulness over rough terrain and in adverse conditions. In his book, *The Bicycle and the Bush*,[15] Jim Fitzpatrick describes how the importance of utilitarian bush cycling has been ignored by Australian historians and by the creators of Outback legend. (He suspects that a similar process may have led

60 The role of the bicycle in the Australian bush has been ignored by the creators of Outback legend. Prospectors relied heavily on their bicycles. They used their own network of rough cycle tracks, or followed the smoother paths made by the Afghan camels which had been imported to carry heavy goods around the goldfields.

to an underestimation of the bicycle's role in rural America.) Coolgardie, a principal Australian gold-mining town, was described in 1896: 'Looking down Bayley Street the first thing noticed by a stranger is the great number of cycles lining both sides of the street, and dodging hither and thither the whole length of this well known thoroughfare, giving it a very modern aspect.' (p. 166)

Bush cyclists undertook long, arduous journeys, sometimes travelling by night to avoid the heat. Prospectors relied heavily on their bicycles, both during goldrushes and as general workhorses. Bicycles were also used by mine managers, surveyors, government officials and visiting journalists. Wherever the Post Office was laggard in servicing new settlements freelance postal and message-taking services were set up by enterprising cyclists, one of whom rode weekly from Coolgardie to Dundas, 280 miles return, equipped with a water bottle, revolver and knife. His fee was a shilling per letter.

The clergymen of the West Australian goldfields cycled round their huge parishes. Probably the first to do so was the Methodist minister of Coolgardie, who wrote to the *Perth Western Mail* in July 1894 beseeching readers to provide him with a bicycle: 'I have no money, it is very scarce here—From outlying places comes the call to me—"Come and help us"—but I am unable to respond to these calls except that I walk distances of thirty to one hundred miles. A good bicycle (none but a good one is any good here) can be delivered to me for about £35.'

The Australian bicycle market was dominated by American and Canadian imports. The typical bush bicycle had no brakes and some riders slowed themselves down on descents by pressing their feet against the front tyre, or by trailing a stick or a branch along the ground—either held in the hand or tied to the bicycle. Thorn punctures were a regular problem and often had to be repaired without water. One trick was to blow tobacco smoke into the inner tube, identifying the puncture hole by noticing where the smoke escaped. If repair was impossible the tyre could be stuffed with grass, rope or strips of hazel, or the bicycle could be 'ridden on the rims', although wooden rims did not always cope well with this latter treatment.

Across in the sheep-raising states of Eastern Australia the bicycle provided transport for gangs of itinerant shearers. The Wolesley Sheep Shearing Machine Co. produced an attachment which, when connected to a bicycle with its rear wheel off the ground, provided power to a hand-held shear.

Women and Cycling

For women the bicycle became a vehicle of liberation from domesticity and isolation. Those who opposed cycling for women, such as Mrs Linton, the elderly American anti-feminist writer, were losing touch with the advancing spirit of the age. She warned that 'chief of all the dangers attending this new development of feminine freedom is the intoxication which comes with unfettered liberty' (*Lady's Realm* June 1896). She was, in fact, opposed to cycling by either sex, describing it as 'a work of penance rather than pleasure'. In the same year the militant Women's Rescue League, based in Washington D.C., was warning that cycling fostered a familiarity with men which led to immorality, and that cycling was so injurious to women that it would render them invalids within a decade. The danger-to-health argument was more usually propagated by male doctors. It was claimed in Paris that 'the bicycle signifies the end of womanhood since its use causes serious damage to the feminine organs of matrimonial necessity.'[16] There was talk of young mothers losing their breast milk as a result of cycling, and of damage to women's nerves. Other objections were more aesthetic in nature: 'Few will contend that the lady cyclist is a thing of beauty. The pedal action is too like the rhythmic swing of a carpet beater, and the addition of dust to a heated face and shapeless garments in no way suggests personal cleanliness.' (*Woman*, 5 June 1890).

The attitude of educated males to women cyclists was, on the whole, approving, but only if 'feminine charm' were maintained. The writer of an 1895 handbook for Austrian cyclists wrote, on the subject of female competitive cyclists, that 'Even though a degree of vanity comes into the matter, we find that a smart lady sporting companion, with a glowing little face and a fetching outfit, is always preferable to a bluestocking.'[17] The principle that women athletes should preserve their femininity was applied to other sports. As late as 1909 Prussian girls who contested the high jump and long jump were judged for their grace and style as well as for length and distance. The restriction or prohibition of female athletics was, of course, common to many countries but was less marked in France where, in cycle sport, they performed for results and were honoured for their achievements. In 1895, for example, Hélène Dutrieu recorded 39.190 kilometres in an hour-event and became the women's record holder. Nevertheless, Pierre de Coubertin, who revived the Olympics in the 1890s, opposed female participation. Female swimmers were not officially admitted until 1912, and female track and field athletes had to wait until 1928.

There was virtually no feminine opposition to the view that physical attractiveness was an indispensible passport to the public acceptance of cycling for women. 'As to the stout person – well, if she will persist in cycling, she must be content to look as well as she can', wrote a female columnist in *Vanity Fair* on the 11 June 1896.

The question of whether women should cycle was quickly outdated by the question of what they should wear while doing so. The late nineteenth century fashion in outdoor clothing was for ankle-length dresses over multitudes of petticoats. Waists were tightly and unhealthily corsetted, and heads weighted down by substantial hats: altogether a restrictive and dangerous outfit for cycling. In France women's cycling was given a head start by the adoption of the knickerbocker costume. This enabled them to ride crossbarred bicycles long before drop-framed machines became generally available, and they rode with more freedom and *joie de vivre* than fashion-fettered Englishwomen. Fashion writers in England, who tended to be conservatively minded ladies of Society, abhorred the Frenchwoman's costume which 'makes her look, if like anything on earth, like an ugly, badly-made little man'.[18] The relationship between the Frenchwoman's choice of dress and her energetic cycling style was perniciously turned on its head by the London and Paris Fashions correspondent of the *Lady's Realm* in September 1897:

61 Hélène Dutrieu, at the age of sixteen. Her bicycle is a minimal, brakeless track machine, equipped with the Simpson Lever Chain, which many wrongly thought gave a mechanical advantage over standard chains. She rode professionally for the makers of the chain. Hélène Dutrieu had an outstanding cycling career before taking to motor sport and aviation. In 1913 she became probably the first female aviator in France, and was awarded the *Légion d'Honneur*.[27]

A bicycling turn-out in Paris is typical of all that is vulgar and ugly, and it is a riddle to our minds to think how a Frenchwoman, so ultra-particular in every respect as regards dress, can mount her bicycle with a knowledge that she is looking her very worst. To be candid, an Englishwoman would wear such a get-up to better advantage, Nature having given her a figure more adapted to such attire. The Parisian is not built for athletic exercise, the Englishwoman is.

Knickerbockers had been invented in the United States in the 1850s. It was only later that Mrs Bloomer was associated with them, and later still that cycling gave a boost to this 'bifurcated nether garment'. American cyclists

62 Various options for the woman cyclist.

63 Mrs Hutton Moss, a Society lady, wearing an outfit which avoids all compromise with common sense. She was well known for her skill at musical figure riding and had performed before royalty. Her Singer is equipped with an electric light which Mrs Hutton Moss designed herself.[28]

were first seen wearing them in the Spring of 1893, and they caused a sensation. A year later newspapers reported that there were nearly a hundred New York women cycling in 'trousers', but mostly under cover of darkness. Self-confidence grew. American women founded their own cycling clubs, for which bloomers were often standard dress, and there were 'bloomer dances' to which only women in bloomers were admitted (with their male companions). Colonel Pope boosted the cause by featuring bloomer-clad women in his cycle adverts. Bloomers also featured in the fashion designers' 1894 collections and they were worn by Society people during their 1894 Season at Newport, Rhode Island. This deflated much middle-class opposition to bloomers, and they were common by 1895. They

103

remained more of a popular novelty away from the Eastern Seaboard, as perhaps shown by the San Francisco restaurant which dressed its waitresses in bloomers. Public figures who cycled for decorative purposes, such as Lillian Russell and Lilly Langtree, disapproved of bloomers. British advocates of the costume preferred the term 'rational dress'.

Progressive thinkers were scathing of the long skirt, for hygenic as well as emancipatory reasons. According to an American writer, 'the long skirt . . . sweeps the filth and infection of the highway into the homes of civilized man, and doubtless is the cause of many an inexplicable case of contagious disease.'[19] Yet British women cyclists, and many others in Europe with the exception of the French, stuck to their long, heavy skirts—often literally so, since sweating was so easily induced. At the same time they were prepared to wear specialised clothing for hunting, tennis and gymnastics. An English ladies' gymnastics team, performing in Dublin in 1898, wore a costume of jersey and knickers, with a short skirt to the knees. But when they turned out for the ensuing musical cycle ride they had changed into ordinary skirts, evidently for fear of upsetting spectators.

The tyranny of the long skirt caused manufacturers to design drop-frame bicycles to accommodate it (an idea first introduced by Denis Johnson, the hobby-horse maker, in 1819). The lack of a top-tube weakened the structure of the frame, and compensatory measures led to a heavier machine. Awkward chain-guards and rear-wheel dress protectors were needed, and women still found it necessary to take such measures as weighing down their skirt hems by filling them with lead shot, or attaching their hems to various fixing points. Long skirts impeded pedalling and caught the wind like a sail. And those who objected to the visual aspects of knickerbockers seemed to have no objection to the sight of a voluminous dress coming down from an eighteen-inch waist and concealing, in the manner of a tea-cosy, much of the bicycle. The wearing of floribund hats, often equipped with veils to keep off the flies, can hardly have enhanced the spectacle. But above all, inappropriate clothing was unsafe. One female cyclist recalled that 'It is an unpleasant experience to be hurled onto stone setts and find that one's skirt has been so tightly wound round the pedal that one cannot get up enough to unwind it.'[20]

The other tyrant of fashion, tight corsetting, was, according to Lady Harburton, President of the Rational Dress Society, a concomitant of the long skirt: 'What can be the true state of intelligence of a creature which deliberately loads itself with quantities of useless material round its legs . . . and then, in order to correct the ugliness of such a dress, squeezes in its body until the vital functions can only be carried on imperfectly?'[21] The Rational Dress Society's proposals for cycling dress—centred on knickerbockers and looser waists—received little support from the CTC, which, like the LAW, was concerned that any such whiff of radicalism would harm the image of the club and of cycling in general. In 1894 the CTC Gazette removed its pro-rational dress ladies' column writer, Lillian Campbell-Davidson and engaged Miss Fanny Erskine, who began by expressing her contempt for 'persons who swagger about in their hybrid costumes'. It was with reluctance that the CTC backed Lady Harburton, one of its members, in a legal action against a public house landlady who had, in October 1898,

64 British women persisted in wearing inappropriate long dresses for cycling. Although the bicycle was a liberating vehicle for women their style of riding and their style of bicycle were both severely restricted by the dictates of fashion in clothes. The wearing of knickerbockers often brought offensive criticism, especially in the North of England.

65 Sixteen year old Tessie Reynolds caused, according to *Cycling*, 'real pain, not unmixed with disgust', when she cycled from Brighton to London and back in 8½ hours in 1893, paced by male friends and wearing a trousered costume. She compromised with convention by sitting on a drop-framed bicycle when being photographed after the event, rather than on the crossbarred bicycle she had used for her ride.

been prepared to serve the rationally dressed Lady in the men's bar but not in the coffee-room. The court found in favour of the landlady but the publicity was considered useful to the Rational Dress cause.

It took considerable courage to wear rational dress in Britain. When sixteen year old Tessie Reynolds rode from Brighton to London and back in September 1893, wearing a trousered costume, she became the subject of impassioned argument in the correspondence columns of the cycling press. Not only had Miss Reynolds worn 'immodest and degrading' dress, she had used a crossbarred bicycle, had been paced by male friends, and had dared to ride strenuously: about 110 miles in 8½ hours. Two years later the (male) cycling correspondent of *The Clarion* wrote: 'Few would believe how insulting and coarse the British public could be unless they had ridden through a populated district with a lady dressed in Rationals. And the poorer the district the more incensed do the people appear.'[22] Few women of the 1890s habitually cycled alone, whatever their choice of costume. Magazines warned of attacks by tramps on lonely roads. In July 1897 *Country Life* claimed that women were particularly vulnerable to 'gangs of roughs ... who have taken up professionally the business of blackmailing cyclists'.

66 Emily and Tom Mott riding a rod-steered tandem in Leicester around 1895. The transmission is fully enclosed and, apart from back-pedalling, the only method of braking seems to have been the then standard plunger brake operated onto the tread of the front wheel.

For the great majority of women the bicycle was not an implement of radicalism but a means of social integration. They cycled with their young men, their husbands and their children. Tandeming became a favourite occupation for couples: Harry Dacre's famous song, 'Daisy Bell' was written in 1892 and its celebration of the 'bicycle made for two' lives on in our popular culture. Tandems created questions of etiquette. It seemed fitting for the man to sit at the front so as to take control and to shield the woman from the wind. Yet it was discourteous to show one's back to a lady and to additionally obscure her view of the scenery. On most early tandems the woman sat in front and steered. But some tandems allowed the man to sit at the rear and yet steer (or help steer) by means of rods attached to the front handlebars.

The Development of Cycle Sport

Although the bicycle brought new freedom and private pleasure to many, its role in the world of sport was increasingly regulated. The chief social characteristics of high bicycle racing in the 1870s and 1880s—quantification of performance, bureaucratisation and class conflict—were intensified in the 1890s. The kind of systematised, regimented, record-hungry sport which the industrialised nations were importing from England depended on specialisation and hierarchical power structures. Cyclists competed with the help or hindrance of trainers, race organisers, handicappers, time-keepers, licence-issuers and governing committee members. The keeping of international records, which began around 1880, made it possible for, say, an Australian cyclist to compete against a Norwegian who had died before the Australian was born. Competitors and spectators became 'sports-numerate'. They fell within the spell of a competitiveness expressed in statistical calculations and tabulated results. They applied themselves, personally or vicariously, to the single-minded pursuit of improved performances measured in fractions of a second.

The movement towards the regularisation of cycle sport engendered national governing bodies for competitive cycling in Britain (1878), France (1881), the USA (1881), the Netherlands (1883), Germany (1884) and Sweden (1900). Interestingly, this was exactly the order in which these countries embarked on their periods of sustained industrialisation, and there is a remarkably similar pattern in the spread of other rationalised sports.[23]

The national organisations which governed cycle sport were often in dispute, largely as a result of their varying attitudes to the spread of professionalism. The Bicycle Union, having quarrelled with the Amateur Athletics Association over cycle race jurisdiction on AAA premises, took issue

67 A wood-surfaced race track in Amsterdam. Many of the spectators are wearing formal dress.

with the Union Vélocipèdique de France over the French body's willingness to allow its 'amateurs' to compete for prizes of up to 2000 francs, the equivalent of about sixteen months pay for a French manual worker. The Bicycle Union often refused to recognise the amateur licences of visiting UVF competitors, and eventually broke off relations on the grounds that the UVF allowed mixed amateur-professional events. The Bicycle Union, renamed the National Cyclists' Union in 1883, made itself unpopular in the early 1890s for its stubborn and seemingly 'nit-picking' opposition to any form of payment whatsoever to riders who professed themselves 'amateur'. For example, in 1891 George Pilkington Mills won the first Paris–Bordeaux race, an event which the French had classed as amateur at the insistence of the British NCU. Knowing that Mills was the works manager at Humber's Beeston factory, the NCU passed a resolution that he be 'asked whether he paid the whole of his expenses in the above-mentioned race'. Mills most probably *had* paid his own way, but the distinction between amateurs and professionals was becoming increasingly clouded by this question of 'makers' amateurism', whereby cycle racing employees of cycle firms could be construed as furthering their employers' interests.

By the mid-1880s the National Cyclists' Union had become alarmed at the perceived dangers of racing on the open road. The police, the press and the public were complaining of large numbers of riders, paced and pacing, hurtling recklessly along public roads. A further development was the establishment of the Roads Record Association, to govern long-distance paced record attempts. In the same year the North Road Cycling Club was established. So great was its activity on the nation's principal road that the *Rational Dress Society Gazette* of January 1895 reported, no doubt exaggeratedly, that 'the North Road really has become a cycling track as well as a public thoroughfare and, indeed, on half holidays and whole holidays it has ceased to be a thoroughfare at all for non-cyclists'. In 1890 the NCU formally proscribed all road events, much to the delight of the CTC. From this date until the end of the Second World War British cycle sport was effectively isolated from Continental developments in road racing, which helps explain Britain's lack of public interest and sporting success in events such as the Tour de France.

British roadmen turned to the introverted and almost masonic sport of time trialling, involving separate, individual performances against the clock. In contrast with the chaos and ballyhoo of a massed road race, time triallists avoided drawing attention to themselves, in the interests of their sport's survival. They used secret codes and arcane directions to identify meeting points, usually on quiet country roads. At the break of dawn, when little traffic was about, they would set off one by one, sombrely dressed in black.

In 1921 the NCU dropped its opposition to time trialling and, in the following year, the Road Racing Council was set up to supervise the sport. It was later renamed the Road Time Trials Council. Time trialling remains popular and still has an air of conspiratorial eccentricity.

Throughout Europe the defenders of amateur cycling were being forced back and often outflanked by a crasser and commercialised professionalism. In the United States the League of American Wheelmen had taken early control of cycle sport but was unable to fend off the many-headed advances of professionalism. In an attempt to maintain standards they tolerated limited professionalism but promoters and riders complained that the LAW suppressed their earnings by banning Sunday events, and by limiting purses and the number of events. In 1893 the National Cycling Association, or 'Cash Prize League' was organised in Philadelphia and established early links with the National Baseball League. There were unfulfilled plans to build cycle tracks around the twelve baseball grounds belonging to the League. The new cycling association did, however, wrest jurisdiction of the big city tracks from the LAW, and the LAW finally renounced control of racing in 1900 with the intention of concentrating on the promotion of good roads. The whole organisation was by this time in the early stages of its demise.

Track events had the advantage of allowing promoters to charge admis-

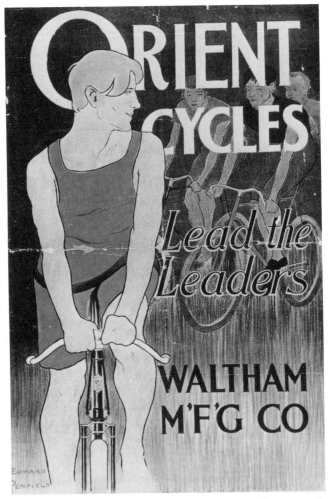

68 A poster by Edward Penfield for an American manufacturer, circa 1895.

sion. They also gave spectators the chance to see more of their heroes: in a road race the cyclists passed only once. Tracks built in Britain in the 1890s rarely met with commercial success, due partly to the tradition of having no sport on Sundays. In France, however, tracks and velodromes took considerable profits and became an important feature of working-class leisure. They were often managed by ex-racing men. Most sporting events took place on a Sunday and many velodromes were used by leisure cyclists and cycle riding schools during the week. One of the first major velodromes in Paris was the Buffalo, the construction of which was financed by the director of the Folies Bergère. The Buffalo was so named since it was built on the site of Buffalo Bill's circus. Around 1896 the velodromes were filled to capacity and the Folies Bergère itself was used for bicycle racing at one point. Some people failed to appreciate the fundamental difference between middle-class leisure cycling and cycling as a commercial spectacle for the working classes. For example, the small town of Choisy-le-Roi, a favourite Sunday cycling destination for Parisians, built a permanent racing track in 1895. The venture flopped, for the inhabitants had not realised that excursionists were out for more pastoral pleasures. Also, devotees of the track, who were often non-cyclists themselves, were not prepared to travel to Choisy-le Roi to watch events.[24]

The professionals of the 1890s were public figures: stars created and cherished by the cycling press. In France the passion for cycle racing supported a daily sports paper, *Le Vélo*, which had a circulation of 80,000 in 1894. The cycle race track was an arena for folk heroes. The public could relate to *géants de la route* drawn from their own class and often from their own town, and it mattered little if their heroes were in the employ of a cycle manufacturer. Furthermore, their heroes were often endearingly small men. British crowds warmed to Jimmy Michael, the first British rider to win a professional world championship, who was little over five foot tall.

Self-employed professionals had to haggle for a living. J. W. Stocks, for example, quarrelled with the promoters of the Goole Sports who had promised him a ten guinea fee but tried, after the event, to fob him off with a medal half that value. There were occasional strikes among professional riders, and last-minute refusals to compete were particularly troublesome since they left promoters with thousands of spectators to placate.

Charles Terront, France's most celebrated professional, showed an unceremonious and often brazen will to win. In 1893, for example, in a 1500 kilometre track competition against his arch-rival Corré, Terront caused a sensation by using, for his *besoins physiologiques*, a rubber inner tube attached to his bicycle frame. From time to time the capacity crowd saw him pass the receptacle to his wife for emptying. Meanwhile, his less imaginative opponent, who was losing valuable time dismounting and running to the nearest urinal, took to the use of a sponge. Cycle sport had come a long way since the decorous days of the gentleman amateurs.

In their 1893 match both Terront and Corré circuited the track behind successive teams of pacers on five- or six-seat multicycles. Such machines, dubbed *artillerie à pédales* in France, became a standard feature of the more important cycle sport events in Europe. A top rider aiming for a fifty mile record would expect six multicycle teams, each on the track for two miles at a time. The pacing teams created 'dead air' for their cyclist. At least one team went as far as having its rearmost rider wear an outdoor coat which he held open wide.[25] Sometimes an additional team rode alongside the soloist to protect him from sidewinds. The point at which multicycles replaced each other was crucial. Any loss of pace as the soloist slipped from behind one wheel to another could destroy his chances of success in a short distance event. Multicycles brought speed and spectacle to events as they drew their soloists high on the straights before swooping down on the curves. Professional multicycle teams were either in the pay of a manufacturer—the Dunlop teams were world famous—or were self-employed. A group of riders would club together to buy a multicycle and then hire themselves out, travelling extensively by train from venue to venue. The job had its dangers. A collision, a broken fork or a snapped chain could bring six men crashing down and, according to one account,[26] some crews were prepared to abandon ship on hearing a tyre blow out.

Multicycles were replaced by motorcycles as soon as the technology became available. Motor pacing was cheaper than employing teams of multicyclists and had novelty value. But many felt that the combustion engine choked the magic out of paced events. Pacing by motor car became permissible in some continental road events such as the annual Bordeaux–Paris race between 1897 and 1899. Whatever the kind of pacing used the true nature of a rider's performance was distorted by the quality of the pacing facilities at his disposal. Only those professionals who had manufacturing sponsors to pay the bills could hope for sustained success in paced events.

The bicycle played an important role in the commercialisation of sport. It also forced the issue of amateur versus professional status, and provided new and exciting spectator events. It had, in turn, been refined by technology in the service of sport, becoming a marvel of grace and efficiency, soon to be available to almost everyone.

69 American multicycle pacers. In the course of an event the solo rider would cycle wheel to wheel with his pacers. A star rider would expect five or six changes of pacing team in the course of a mile record attempt, each change-over to be executed with the greatest of skill.

6
THE SOCIETY CYCLING BOOM
AND
WORKING-CLASS ASPIRATIONS

The Society Vogue

BY 1896 THE PASSION for safety cycling had reached far beyond North West Europe and the United States. Excitement and curiosity had been carried abroad by cycle-loving diplomats and colonials, by the hectic enterprise of manufacturers, and by the influence of London and Paris fashion on the international middle class. The extent of the vogue is suggested by John Foster Fraser's travelogue, *Round the World on a Wheel*. Fraser describes how, in 1896, he and his two companions were escorted by cyclists from Budapest, and later by the wheelmen of Nyireghaza (North East Hungary), who rode with giant sunflowers on their bicycles' headsets. In India they cycled with colonial dignitaries and in Japan they were welcomed by the Unreliable Wheelmen of Yokohama, a club composed of 'Scotsmen and humorists'. Had he taken a more northerly route Fraser would have encountered the five thousand cyclists of St Petersburg or the members of the Moscow Society of Velocipede Lovers. To the south he would have been welcomed by the colonial wheelers of Johannesburg, by the Sultan of Zanzibar, who was to become one of Raleigh's best customers, or by the Ameer of Kabul, who had, in that euphoric year of 1896, ordered bicycles for the ladies of his hareem. New markets were also being created in Latin America and Japan by American cycle manufacturers. Reports of cycling activity at the very outposts of Western civilisation were relayed back to the self-congratulatory cycling public of the industrialised nations.

1896 was also the year in which cycling soared to a height of popularity among the middle classes of the motherlands themselves. Britain and France had about a million cyclists each, Germany had half a million, and estimates for the USA range from two to four million. The phenomenon has become known as the 'cycling craze': not primarily because of its numerical or geographical extent, but because of the high pitch of excitement. In the following three decades numbers of cyclists were to rise five-fold, in Britain and France at least, yet never again was the bicycle to catch the public imagination so spectacularly.

The craze in Britain was particularly infectious in 1895 and 1896. CTC membership rose from 16,343 to 34,655, the Prince of Wales bought a

70 The Nizam of Hyderabad's Bicycle Boys' Corps parading past their sovereign in 1895. They were attached to the Hyderabad Imperial Service troops.

tricycle, and George Bernard Shaw, who declared cycling to be 'a capital thing for a literary man', could be seen wobbling around the London parks. The lanes of Surrey filled with wheeling day-trippers, Thomas Cook was planning organised cycle tours of the continent, and the likes of John Foster Fraser were adventuring across the world on their Rovers, Humbers and Rudges. Sales of cycling magazines reached all-time records, many new publications fluttered onto the market and general interest magazines began to carry cycling columns. The bicycle was well in tune with the rhythms of the 1890s. Holbrook Jackson was later to describe the period as 'an era of hope and action' which was characterised by 'the feeling of expectancy, born not alone of a mere toying with novel ideas, but due also to a determination to taste new sensation, for the sake of personal development'. (*The 1890s*, 1913)

The craze encouraged optimism among entrepreneurs and capital investment in cycle companies rose from around £5,000,000 in 1895 to £14,000,000 in 1896. According to census returns the number of 'cycle makers' rose from 22,241 in 1895 to 46,039 in 1897. Rapid growth was also helped by the industry's ability to draw labour from related trades and by the readiness of many firms to take up cycle making in place of, or alongside, their normal business. The Birmingham Small Arms Co. (BSA) had entered the cycle trade in the 1880s and became a major supplier of lugs, fittings and bicycles to other manufacturers. Among the more temporary converts were the Wolesley Sheep Shearing Co. of Birmingham, Palmers Shipbuilding of Jarrow and Armstrongs Ordinance Works of Newcastle upon Tyne. The BSA cycle plant had grown to ten acres by 1896, and in the same year Raleigh built a new seven-and-a-half acre factory in Nottingham and 312 new cycle companies were founded. This surging vigour was not matched by growth in other industries and, with the possible exception of breweries, was the first instance of organised capital investment in the field of mass leisure.

One peculiarly British aspect of the craze was first noticed in Battersea Park, West London, in the Spring of 1895. The aristocracy had finally begun to cycle, but in their own inimitable way. The scene was later to be described by Jerome K. Jerome:

> In Battersea Park, any morning between eleven and one, all the best blood in England could be seen, solemnly peddling up and down the half-mile drive that runs between the river and the refreshment kiosk. But these were the experts—the finished article. In shady bypaths, elderly countesses, perspiring peers, still at the wobbly stage, battled bravely with the laws of equilibrium; occasionally defeated, they would fling their arms round the necks of hefty young hooligans who were reaping a rich harvest as cycling instructors: 'Proficiency guaranteed in twelve lessons'. Cabinet Ministers, daughters of a hundred Earls might be recognised by the initiated, seated on the gravel, smiling feebly and rubbing their heads.[1]

Most of the park practitioners were women, exhibiting leg-of-mutton sleeves, hour-glass waists and enveloping skirts. Nor were their bicycles spared this triumph of taste. They were multi-coloured: pink with white lines, lemon with green lines; anything but black. Some were even painted to match the colour scheme of the lady's dress, and some male riders had their machines liveried in their regimental colours. Such fashion was rarely seen on the roads outside the parks, since aristocrat and bicycle, the latter wrapped in a tasteful bag, were usually transported there by carriage. 'I don't ride in London', explained Lady Colin Campbell, 'at least not in the streets, with omnibus horses breathing down the back of your neck. In my opinion it is most unfitting for women to expose themselves to the dangers of London traffic. Think how London is built—comparatively speaking, there is not a wide thoroughfare in it; and then consider the vehicles, the huge two-horse wagons and so on. It really is not fair to the drivers to cycle in town.'[2] By the following Spring, of 1896, cycling was permissible in Hyde Park, on the doorstep of Mayfair, thanks to aristocratic pressures exerted through the Cyclists' Touring Club. Whereas Battersea Park cyclists could be counted in their hundreds in 1895, there were two or three thousand

71 Ladies saw their bicycles as an enhancement to elegance and took them along to the photographer's, in spic-and-span condition, for the annual portrait. In this picture the open frame, chaincase and dress-guard on the rear wheel all testify to the tyranny of the long dress, although the lady here is dressed for her photograph and not for cycling.

72 Decorated bicycles at a country gymkhana.

awheel in fashionable Hyde Park on fine mornings the following year, and further social and decorative refinements had been devised over the winter.

Park cycling became popular around the Empire. A resident of Rangoon, in Burma, was later to recall that, 'There was a time when from six to eight o'clock every morning, between *chota hazri* and breakfast, a hundred Englishmen and Englishwomen might have been encountered in the course of one's morning run round the delightful paths of the Royal Lakes, that fairyland of tropical colour, set off by the majestic golden spire of the Great Pagoda'. (*CTC Gazette*, August 1901)

Most of the Hyde Park cyclists were in London for the Summer Season, an intensive round of dress balls, garden parties, receptions, carriage outings and the like. During the cycling craze events such as these were often adapted to include an element of cycling, and many an invitation card had a 'Bring your bicycle' across the bottom. Wealthy families parked their cycles ornamentally in their wide hallways, and some employed uniformed boys to take charge of visitors' bicycles and clean them. W. S. Gilbert, associate of Sullivan, kept a fleet of seven quality bicycles and employed a groom to tend them.

Cyclists began to accompany fox hunts. 'At almost every meet now may be seen a detachment of cyclists', wrote Fanny Erskine in *Badminton Magazine*[3] (the same Fanny Erskine who replaced the rather too radical Lillian Campbell-Davidson as women's columnist on the *CTC Gazette*). For a while the bicycle usurped the horse at country club gymkhanas. When the upper classes cycled at gymkhana or charity events they adhered to two motifs: the floral and the military. There were competitions in decorating bicycles with flowers; cyclists plaited a flower-hung maypole by cycling round it, and there was much general throwing about of flowers. On the other hand there were mock cavalry charges, tilting at rings, tent pegging and 'cleaving the Turk's head'. One event combined both elements: the cycling battle of flowers. Musical figure riding became a staple on such occasions and Miss Stuart Snell trained ladies in the art each Friday in the Albert Hall, with friends and spectators welcome. They practised 'figure threading', 'reverse circles', throwing soft balls while riding and square

73 Musical riding for charity at the Crystal Palace in 1899, probably one of the last such rides to take place. Typically, the ladies' performance combined the military with the floral. As in tennis, musical riding costumes were white: perhaps betokening purity, or an innocence of the oily, mechanical nature of their bicycles. It may also have served as a mark of their affluence: these ladies could afford a special costume, and the laundry bills that went with it.

dances such as the 'Lancers' and the 'Caledonian'. The ladies performed at the wedding of Princess Maud and Prince Carl (who had courted one another on royal cycle outings) and, according to Miss Stuart Snell, 'The Prince of Wales liked it very much . . . and the dancers—if you can call them so—bowed to the Princess as they passed on their machines, and so, for a second, the machines were actually still. All my riders were dressed in white, on flower-decked machines, and cycled to the music of the Hungarian Band'.[4] Miss Stuart Snell's ladies rode American Columbias, which had high bottom brackets, making pedals less likely to strike the ground. One of London Society's Australian off-shoots was especially keen on musical riding. The first vice-regal ball of the 1896 Season in Melbourne began with a musical ride, in Court dress, in the ballroom. It was in 1896 that Major Walter Wingfield of the Queen's Body-Guard of Gentlemen-at-Arms, inventor of lawn tennis, published his *Bicycle Gymkhana and Musical Rides*, which, among other things, listed standard commands: 'Serpentine down the centre', 'Go large' and 'Retire from both flanks'. He described how to ride in formations which depict the initials of the host, and how to conduct the polo race: whilst riding a bicycle one used a golf club to polo a tennis ball around croquet sticks; an event which comprised all five of the upper classes' favourite sports. Wingfield's suggestion for one event was to 'ride slowly by on your bicycle with a revolver, at fifteen feet distance, and put the six bullets into the Turk's head while passing . . . Considering the crisis in the East this is good practice.'

The wealthy British enjoyed their new hobby on holiday and found that it complemented another technological artifact of leisure: the photographic camera. A tourist travelling with her sister on the French Riviera was later to recall: 'It was delightful skimming along on our bicycles, I with my Bullseye Kodak attached to the carrier in front of me so that whenever any little group of animals or peasants took my fancy I had nothing to do but jump off and take a snap shot. We were in the fashion with our bicycles; the billiard room at the Hôtel St Bartélemy was turned into a bicycle stable and crammed with machines of every make and grade belonging to the various visitors.'[5]

Back home exclusive cycle clubs were established in West London mansions. The Wheel Club, which opened in South Kensington, was a paradigm of luxury inside, and its outside facilities were described thus in *The Lady's Realm*:

The extensive gardens . . . have been threaded with a wooden cycle track, conveniently shaded by ancestral trees and commanding a charming vista of flower beds; and the fair cyclists have a continuous concert of nature's songsters during the morning hours, when this is reserved for their sole use. Skilled instructors of both sexes are there to support the wavering, who, should the weather be unpropitious, can resort to the covered riding school. The stables of this old mansion are entirely given over to the horse of wheels . . . and the harness room has been turned into a cycle-repairing shop. The great feature of the club are its summer social gatherings, when the grounds, tastefully illuminated, and thronged with beauty, on and off wheels, are a gay scene . . . At the musical rides the ladies are trained by an army man to ride to military music.

This piece appeared in September 1897, and mentions elsewhere that the club was about to set up 'some thirty or so branch-houses at the fashionable cycling resorts outside London'. There were other signs of confidence that the craze would last. The Chaperon Cycling Association was formed in 1896 and offered escorts for ladies at 3s 6d per hour or 10s 6d per day. Chaperons had to provide their own bicycles. Riding schools were set up in large numbers and the cycle trade foresaw endless expansion. There were, for example, over twenty cycle shops in Holborn Viaduct, the centre of the up-market London cycle trade, although quality bicycles were in short supply.

In August 1896 *The Hub*, a magazine aimed specifically at women cyclists, reported somewhat haplessly in its first issue that Hyde Park was devoid of cyclists. By the Spring of 1897 it was becoming clear that the Society cycling boom was losing momentum. The cycling magazines seemed to have run out of original things to say and were reduced to such matters as personality profiles, and repetitive advice on riding technique. By the beginning of the 1898 cycling season it had to be admitted that the notables of London were abandoning cycling just as they had abandoned ice skating at the Princess Skating Club eight years before. The park cycling ceremony had not only become boring, but was too easily gatecrashed: any upstart from Bayswater could turn up with a bicycle. Besides, cycling was tiring and sometimes it rained. Some aristocrats continued to cycle round their country estates but the mania for exclusive novelties was to remain dormant till the motor car arrived on the scene.

The socialite cyclists of Mayfair and Belgravia had waited till the cyclists' struggle for status had been largely won before venturing out themselves. They did, however, add their undoubted prestige to the cause of cycling and decisively established women's right to cycle whatever the social level.

The cycle craze in France had started earlier than its British counterpart and French cyclists faced fewer social constraints. Polite society cycled in the Bois de Boulogne. Although Bois cycling was a social event, and well reported at that, it was different in many respects from its Hyde Park equivalent. There was no sudden High Society craze. Cyclists began to fill the Bois around 1892 and could be counted in their thousands well beyond 1896. They were prepared to cycle energetically and to enjoy themselves.

74 Lady Idena Brassey, in 1896, looking distinctly radical in her mannish cycling outfit. Not for her the restricted waist, nor the leg-of-mutton sleeves which hit a height of fashion in that year. She does not seem, however, to be wearing a divided skirt, not to mention knickerbockers.

75 A tandem in the Bois de Boulogne. Cyclists rendezvoused at the edge of the park before setting off along the long tree-lined avenues, from which amusement areas, restaurants, cycle club headquarters and cycle hire *dépôts* were offset.

There was a greater social mix: students, artists, bourgeois, government ministers, and even the President of France, Casimir-Perier, who tandemed round the Bois each morning with his wife and children. Even members of the old French aristocracy cycled with gusto. The *beau monde* of Paris were not the only Bois cyclists. There was also the *demi-monde*, a mysterious class of ostentatiously wealthy kept women. Actresses were also leading arbiters of fashion. Perhaps the most heavily reported Bois rider was Sarah Bernhardt, a heroine of that ambiguous morality which so delighted the Paris of the *Belle Époque*.

The Bois de Boulogne was both bigger and more discreet than Hyde Park. Cyclists could rendezvous at the outskirts: at the Brasserie de L'Espérance or at the Chalet du Cycle at Suresnes, where a man made a living pushing other people's bicycles up the hill. In the Bois itself there were tree-shaded, acacia-bordered avenues of asphalt from which cycle club headquarters, restaurants and amusement areas were offset. Some cycled through the Bois and then along the glorious riverside roads to lunch at St Germain or Neuilly. Carriages dropped their passengers off at cycle *dépôts* from which stored bicycles were collected, or at the *ménages* where cycles could be hired. On Sundays regular wheelers shared their pleasures with those who were enjoying their one day off in the week. The atmosphere was that of a carnival and Sunday cycle dress was so bizarre that it became a tourist attraction. As early as 1892 the Prince de Sagin delighted onlookers by riding his 'little steel fairy' while wearing a loud striped suit and a specially designed boater. The Prince was an ardent cyclist and liked to joke that if

76 The invasion of England by American tourists.

77 An alternative to the Bois de Boulogne, especially in bad weather, was provided by the elegant indoor velodromes of Paris. The most prestigious was the Palais-Sport, just off the Champs Elysées. It had three-quarters of a mile of track spiralling down to ground level, immense floor space, luxurious dressing- and bathrooms, a concert hall, a theatre and storage facilities for 800 bicycles. A course of lessons cost twelve francs for men and fifteen for women, since women were judged to need longer to learn.

one *must* run down a pedestrian it should never be a man from one's own club, and if one *had* to fall it should always be to the Right and not to the Left.[6] At dusk the Sunday revellers festooned their machines with purloined flowers and Chinese lanterns, and those who cycled home made the roads come alive with lantern lights bobbing into the distance.

The bicycle, '*la petite reine*', joined the Parisian extravaganza of public display, frivolity and self-indulgence. They were heady days, at least for the leisured property owners of the city. Whether in a theatre box or on a bicycle it was important to be seen, to perform and to sparkle. There was a considerable amount of cycling in the city streets. The students and advanced spirits of Montmartre and the Latin Quarter were happy to dodge through the traffic, and supervised cycle parking was provided at university faculties, department stores and public offices. Some *concierges* and street corner boot-shiners developed a side-line in cycle supervision.

The bicycle also made its mark on the lives and works of artists and writers. Renoir was frustrated in mid-career when he fell off his bicycle and broke his arm. Toulouse-Lautrec, too crippled to cycle himself, enjoyed the company of racing cyclists at the Vélodrome Buffalo and the Vélodrome de la Seine, both establishments being directed by Lautrec's close friend, the impresario Tristan Bernard. Lautrec produced very few posters for cycle manufacturers. The bicycle craze coincided with advances in poster-printing technology and with the proliferation, primarily in France, of luxuriously colourful advertising posters, many of which promoted tyres, bicycles and velodromes. Idealised and even goddess-like women were portrayed in suggestive proximity to bicycles and the use of erotic, mythological and allegorical themes gave products an aura of fantasy, exoticism and even grandeur, as well as revealing a classical bias in the artists' education.[7]

Many of the avant-garde community of writers and artists saw the bicycle as a synthesiser of art and life, or at least took pleasure in the aesthetic fusion of body and machine. The artist Ferdinand Léger wrote: 'A bicycle operates in the realm of light. It takes control of legs, arms and body, which move on it, by it and under it. Rounded thighs become pistons, which rise or fall, fast or slow.' (*The Circus.*) Alfred Jarry, best known for his chaotic *Ubu Roi* plays, was the most committed cyclist of them all. He described the bicycle as an 'external skeleton' which allowed mankind to outstrip the processes of biological evolution. Jarry was an outrageous eccentric and a wild cyclist. He was no Bois de Boulogne buff, and counterpointed the public obsession with Bois fashions by wearing at all times the tight and gaudy costume of a professional racing cyclist. Jarry caused a stir by wearing it at the funeral of the revered poet Mallarmé, after having followed the cortège on his bicycle. He did make one concession at the funeral of his close friend Marcel Schwob: he pulled his trouser bottoms out of his stockings. He habitually rode round Paris with two revolvers tucked in his belt and a carbine across his shoulder. Some sources say he fired off shots to warn of his approach. It is known for certain, however, that in his maturer days he fixed a large bell from a tram car onto his handlebars. At night he kept his bicycle at the foot of his bed and cycled round the room on it during the day. He died in poverty at the age of thirty-four as a result of malnutrition and absinthe abuse. His literary works include a scandalous magazine article, 'The Passion considered as an Uphill Bicycle Race', and also 'The Ten Thousand Mile Race',[8] in which the five-man crew of a multicycle, bound by rods to their machine, hurtle across Europe and Asia in a grotesque race against an express train. Paced by jet cars and flying machines they reach speeds of 300 kilometres an hour thanks to their diet of Perpetual Motion Food, a volatile mixture of alcohol and strychnine. One of the riders dies of an overdose whilst in the saddle, an event hardly noticed in the farcical pandemonium of technology. The android cyclists of the Perpetual Motion Race have been interpreted as a prophesy of the mechanisation and commercialisation of sport.

78 Alfred Jarry, surrealist writer, and a committed but eccentric cyclist. He became notorious in Paris for his imaginative cycling style and rode his beloved *Clément* track racing machine day in day out on the streets of the city. He also rode it around his cramped lodgings.

79 A firemen's quadricycle from Dressler's Aurora Cycle Works, Breslau. On arriving at a fire they pedalled to pump water through the hose.

80 One of the taxi-tricycles, invented by 'Direktor Hoffman', which were introduced to the streets of Berlin in 1896. They could travel at twice the speed of a Category One horse taxicab, and all journeys were metred. There were hundreds of tricycle-taxis in Berlin two years later.

Not all writers had cause to welcome the bicycle. When Léon Bloy complained to his publisher that his books were not selling the latter retorted: 'What do you expect? Ever since people went mad about cycling they've had no time for reading.'

In Germany the sophisticated middle classes of the big cities did not allow their governments' restrictions to exclude them from the international craze. In Berlin, where one in four of the electorate owned a bicycle, cyclists supported their own candidates in municipal elections. This kind of pressure resulted in nearly all the roads of the Capital becoming accessible to cyclists in February 1896. German interest in cycles designed for special purposes intensified and in 1898 a magazine reported, perhaps with some exaggeration, that 500 tricycle taxicabs were plying the streets of Berlin.[9]

The fashionable illustrated magazines of Italy and Spain reveal no great fascination for leisure cycling, and a British cycling visitor to Spain considered the heavy import duty on bicycles to be the chief restraint. Nevertheless Spaniards took passionately to cycling as a spectator sport and six cycle sport magazines were published in Madrid.

The cycle craze jubilated through the smaller nations of Northern Europe. Denmark took to cycling at a very early stage and Copenhagen was teeming with cyclists by 1895. The Danish royal family's stays at Fredensborg Castle became the excuse for an informal kind of cycling club for the princes and princesses of Europe, initiated by the Czarevitch Nicholas of Russia. The older members of the Danish royal family enjoyed attending public cycle races.

In the riding schools of Amsterdam, which were probably the best in Europe, novices could be coached by splendidly uniformed instructors. Helpers steadied cyclists by means of leather waist bands, and walls were covered with protective padding. There was often a pianist to jollify proceedings. *La Vie en Rose* was particularly popular but the hit song of 1896 was *Allemaal op de Fiets* (Everyone on your Bike), a singalong from a highly successful musical. At one point in the song the audience shout out simple replies to the singer's questions:

> What gives you courage and muscles of steel?
> The bike! The bike! The bike!
> What gives your hinges that supple feel?
> The bike! The bike! The bike!
> What's the subject of all conversations?
> The bike! The bike! The bike!
> What puts us Dutch ahead of all nations?
> The bike! The bike! The bike!

81 The Vesterbrogade riding school in Denmark. In the 1890s a whole generation of adults suddenly needed to be taught how to balance on two wheels.

What makes all the classes dress alike?
The bike! The bike! The bike!
What makes a gent of your labouring tyke?
The bike! The bike! The bike![10]

A cycle boom affected the upper classes of the United States in the mid-1890s. New York City's 'Four Hundred', the self-defining social élite, formed the Michaux Cycle Club in 1895, with headquarters on upper Broadway. The club's social evenings and gymkhana were, as in England, occasions for elaborate set pieces. In the 'Balaclava Mêlée', for example, four male cyclists wearing fencing masks used canes to strike at plumes fixed to each other's headgear. For the ladies there was serpentining down lines of bowling pins and both sexes took part in cycling versions of dances such as the 'Virginia Reel'. Members began to ride out in groups to breakfast at an inn on Riverside Drive, or to the Westchester Country Club for dinner. There were other élite clubs in New York City, such as the Metropolitan, which kept 200 bicycles on hand for its members. Society cycled in Central Park. Many moved to their mansions in Newport for the Summer Season, where, joined by the *beau monde* of other Eastern cities, they could cycle in

82 Norwegian cyclists on tour around 1901, carrying their luggage on the handle-bars, as was usual. The popularity of cycling reached the middle classes of virtually every western nation.

83 Gretchen and James Hetzel who set off from St Louis in April 1900 to cycle around the world. They survived being attacked and wounded by Bedouins. There had been a long tradition of sponsored round-the-world journeys by American cyclists, begun by Thomas Stevens on his Columbia high-wheeler in the mid-1880s. Public opinion turned against the activity when a Mr Lenz, sponsored by *Outings* magazine, was murdered in Armenia.

a more exclusive milieu. William K. Vanderbilt provided bicycles at his Newport mansion for guests who had formerly been content with horses.

J. D. Rockefeller was not a keen cyclist himself but presented bicycles to friends whose state of health caused him concern. Such members of the established rich preferred a sober style of bicycle, bought from stock. The brasher newly rich, such as Diamond Jim Brady, went for ostentation. Wanting ten gold-plated bicycles to present to his friends, Brady had his own gold-plating plant built, had the job done, and the plant was torn down again. He gave his girlfriend, the celebrated comic opera singer Lillian Russell, a gold-plated bicycle with her monogram engraved on every gold part. It had mother of pearl handlebars, an enormous amethyst on the headset, and spokes encrusted with precious stones. The machine, then valued at $10,000, travelled with her in a plush-lined morocco leather case. Brady shared his fondness for ostentatious machines with the more despotic royal households of the world. Democratically elected heads of state, such as William McKinley in the United States and Félix Faure in France, rode appropriately plain machines.

As in other countries, American Society's infatuation with cycling drew disproportionate publicity, and must be seen as part of a more general boom. It was in the already congested cities that the swarms of new cyclists forced themselves onto the nation's attention. They crowded onto the few city streets which had been asphalted or macadamised. In 1897 an estimated 25,000 cyclists used just one such road in New York City on one day. The accident rate soared in city centres and frictions developed, leading to some fierce fist fights between wheelmen and draymen. Cyclists often scorched through traffic at speeds well beyond the 10 m.p.h. which most authorities had allotted them. The city council of Washington D.C. tried to tame scorchers by legislating that no dropped handlebars should extend more than four inches below the level of the saddle.

American cyclists seem to have been pre-occupied by speed and mobility. Their attitudes have been described by Professor Richard Harmond:

> It was not strange that Americans had come to associate speed with the progress of civilization. A mobile, energetic and enterprising people, they knew that swift transportation and communication had been indispensable to the unification and exploitation of their huge and productive land. They had also witnessed the material achievements of such rapidly functioning devices as the sewing machine, typewriter and high-speed press. It may be, too, that, at a different level of consciousness, speed and the closely related desire to save time had become important goals to Americans because, as a people, they were increasingly more concerned with temporal events, rather than those which were to take place in eternity. At any rate, by the 1890s Americans were captivated by the idea of speed, and much of the attraction of the bicycle stemmed from the fact that the vehicle was able to actualize this idea in a highly gratifying fashion.[11]

The bicycle's popularity was borne along by that optimism, imaginativeness and enterprise which was so peculiarly American, and which induced Thomas Edison to prophesy that, before long, hundreds of miles of cycle path would be equipped with overhead cables supplying power to electric motors mounted on bicycles below. Elevated cycle paths were planned, and some were built; stores and theatres organised cycle storage, and new houses were designed with wheel-rooms included. Private enterprise sought out every opening for profit. In New York City the House to House Cleansing Co. smartened up customers' bicycles for a set fee; dime-operated air pumps for cyclists were placed at roadsides. There were myriads of accessories and new inventions. Lillian Russell acquired a Plaster-cast Self-adjusting Nature-Fitting Saddle, cast according to the shape made by her bottom as she sat and pedalled on the manufacturer's dummy saddle, which was covered in an inch of clay. One inventor proposed hanging a magnet forward of the front wheel so as to pick up tacks and nails before they caused a puncture. One firm noticed that widows in mourning did not cycle. So it produced a totally black machine which showed no nickel or shining steel, claiming that it was 'approved for mourning etiquette'. At the other extreme the bicycle invaded the world of entertainment. In Buffalo Bill's Wild West Show Annie Oakley demonstrated her sharpshooting while riding a bicycle instead of a horse, and Professor Bilbo's Olympic Mounted Bicycle Band graced carnivals in the New York area.

The bicycle was taken seriously as a utility vehicle for the public services. The telephone companies put inspectors and line-boys on bicycles to patrol the dense webs of overhead cables which enmeshed the cities. The Chicago ambulance service introduced a cycle ambulance consisting of two tandems in parallel carrying between them a covered box with a stretcher on it. It proved to be faster than any horse vehicle, a three mile run through the city taking sixteen minutes. New York City mounted over 100 street cleansing inspectors on bicycles and the Salvation Army had bicycle corps in New York and Chicago, as well as a touring cycle troupe for the Colorado mining districts.[12]

84 A riding school in the United States which dispensed with instructors and their assistants.

There was much discussion on the effects of the cycling craze on other aspects of the US economy. Tailors, shoemakers, barbers, cigar makers, saloon keepers and street car companies all complained that their trade was being made to suffer. But it was the piano manufacturers who seem to have been worst hit, their trade falling by as much as fifty per cent as customers diverted their cash and time to cycling.[13]

The American cycle industry had boomed at a time of general economic depression. In 1896 about 250 major cycle factories produced well over a million bicycles, and 600 makers of accessories gave work to 60,000 employees. It all represented a combined investment of seventy-five million dollars, which needed to be recouped by huge turn-overs. Manufacturers accordingly encouraged annual design obsolescence supported by gimmickry and hyperbole. The trade-in became a feature of the dealer's business. But in 1897 home-based demand was dropping and production fell by a third. Competition forced prices down to levels which put thirty-five per cent of manufacturers out of business, and sent many of the rest into a series of hasty mergers resulting in the formation of the American Bicycle Company, which even Colonel Pope's flair and energy could not save from eventual liquidation in 1901 (despite the fact that 1,200,000 bicycles had been produced the previous year, a number which equalled that of the boom year of 1896). Tumbling prices diluted the bicycle's prestige but immeasurably increased its use among the lower paid. The aviators Wilbur and Orville Wright, minor cycle makers of Dayton Ohio, sold their cheaper models for eighteen dollars, about the cost of a ready-made suit of clothes.[14]

Wheels for the Workers

Even before the great fall in American prices British manufacturers had been losing international trade to US exports. Agents and customers abroad had come to resent the British cycle trade's delayed deliveries, arbitrary pricing policies and unwillingness to adapt their products to specific markets. British makers clung to a misguided belief that quality would always sell, and that there existed an endless national and international market for prestigious machines destined for fashionable clienteles. The end of the cycling vogue among the wealthy, combined with a flood of cheap American imports, caught manufacturers over-capitalised and unprepared to aim their products down-market. Rudge-Whitworth were the first leading company to react. In July 1897 they reduced their standard cycle from twenty pounds to twelve guineas, and other firms slowly and resentfully followed suit. Prices continued to fall until the First World War: partly due to the shift towards a mass market, but also to substantial changes in production methods. The most striking advances were liquid brazing, which gave

85 Young cyclists in the north of England, around 1900. Falling prices were bringing bicycles within the eager reach of the skilled working classes. Most working-class buyers were young bachelors on regular incomes.

stronger frame joints with less labour, and sheet-steel pressing, both innovations coming from America. There was also the electrification of factories and the increased use of de-skilling automated machinery. Shift work became common and relatively cheap female labour was brought in. On top of all this there were repeated falls in the cost of frame tubing, tyres and chains.[15] British cycles came close to the price of American imports, while being far more reliable. By the turn of the century the industry had saved itself, seen off the 'American Invasion' and brought prices to within the eager reach of the better-off working classes.

The fall in prices did not suddenly mean that everyone in Britain could afford a bicycle. In 1901 a standard bicycle would cost around nine pounds, when the best paid manual workers earned around a pound per week. Even when the average price fell to four pounds, in 1909, working-class buyers needed hire purchase schemes, and sometimes formed clubs to buy their cycles on contract or by mutual guarantee. But bicycles were at last coming into the hands of those who had the greatest need for cheap and independent mobility. Most working-class buyers were young batchelors on regular incomes, and the club runs which took them out of the grimy cities were essentially male affairs.

In his study on working-class isolation and mobility in rural Dorset, P. J. Perry found that intra-parochial working-class marriages decreased from 77 per cent before 1887 to 41 per cent between 1907 and 1916. Marriages to partners living six to twelve miles away increased from 3 per cent to 9 per cent. Perry attributes this new courtship mobility largely to the bicycle: few courting males had the energy to walk six or more miles after a long and strenuous working day. But Perry recognises that the horizons of the rural working classes were also widened by more general social improvements such as increases in leisure and literacy:

> Although the advent of the bicycle may be regarded as the key factor in this rural revolution it is equally clear that several factors operated closely together. It was his higher wage which enabled the labourer to buy the machine and the local newspaper; his literacy enabled him to use the latter to read advertisements for bicycles and of local events, his shorter working week gave him time for such journeys, for reading, and perhaps for writing letters (p. 134).

In 1923 a Dutch historian of cycling described the similar benefits of his country's network of cycle paths: 'Just how useful cycle paths have been in the intellectual development of country people is beyond calculation, but together with the bicycle and the acetylene lantern, which made it possible to take lessons and to attend courses and meetings, they fulfilled a leading role in the intellectual development of the farming population.'[16]

132

In France there were about four million bicycles in circulation by 1914. There was a strong tendency for the skilled urban working classes to set up competition-oriented cycle clubs, being perhaps influenced by the huge popularity of professional racing and its strength as a spectator sport. Among the earliest such clubs were the Societé des Cyclistes Coiffeurs-Parfumeurs (1896) and the Union Cyclistes des Postes et des Télégraphes (1897). Organisations such as the Handlebar Club of the Workers of Corbeil, and the Workers' Pedal Club were founded in the later 1890s.[17]

In Germany cheaper cycle prices encouraged the vigorous growth of the Workers' Cycling Federation, Solidarity (Arbeiterradfahrbund: Solidarität), founded in 1896, whose members quickly earned the description 'Red Hussars of the Class Struggle' as a result of their propaganda and electioneering activities. They organised cycle parades and distributed leaflets, calling themselves the 'Enlightenment Patrols of Social Democracy'. One method of evading identification in those years of repression was to throw handfuls of leaflets at crowds as one cycled quickly past. District branches organised cycle runs and, unlike middle-class clubs, took account of the workers' often restrictive patterns of employment. The Berlin branch had separate sections for night shift workers, bakers and hotel workers, as well as twelve area sections. By 1913 the Workers' Cycling Federation had an impressive 150,000 members, a chain of co-operatively organised cycle shops, a co-operative cycle factory in Offenbach and a circulation of 167,000 for its fortnightly newspaper *The Worker-Cyclist*.[18] This corporate strength was built up despite energetic state repression of all the working-class sports organisations which were set up in the 1890s in reaction and opposition to state-friendly, middle-class sporting bodies. Repression took the form of blacklists, infiltration by spies and straightforward proscription. The members of the Workers' Gymnastics Federation practised in hidden yards and back rooms, and in Berlin the workers' swimming clubs, along with other members of the proletariat seeking recreation, were kept from the city's lakes by constant police patrols. Leading Social Democrat politicians paid little attention to the workers' sporting activities, calling them 'diversions from the class struggle'.

The Workers' Cycling Federation was ideologically averse to offering valuable cups and prizes at its sports meetings, and thereby lost some competitors to middle-class cycling events, where the prizes could be substantial. This put the middle-class clubs, at national and local level, into a quandary. They were ideologically committed to encourage the working classes to develop their bodies on behalf of the Fatherland, but were upset at seeing their prizes carried off by sturdy newcomers, many of whom 'trained' daily on heavyweight delivery cycles.[19]

The Workers' Cycling Federation's British counterpart was the Clarion Cycling Club, which was founded on a national basis in 1895 and reached a maximum membership of around 8000 before being incapacitated by the First World War. The club was born of the Clarion Fellowship, a sporting and charitable socialist movement, which was in turn born of the radical *Clarion* newspaper, founded in 1891. The Clarion movement as a whole offered a compassionate, popularised and by no means scientific form of socialism. It emphasised outdoor leisure pursuits: fellowship and fresh air, away from the cities. A leading Clarionette wrote: 'I claim that the frequent contrasts the cyclist gets of the beauties of nature and the dirty squalor of the towns makes him more anxious than ever to abolish the present system.'[20] In 1941 the historian R. K. Ensor was to write, rather patronisingly, that the files of the Clarion movement's newspaper 'mirror admirably their hobbies and ideals ... cycling, literature, music, arts-and-crafts, "rational" dress, feminism, vegetarianism and back-to-the-land—all gaily jostling one another in a generous and Utopian atmosphere of socialist enthusiasm'.[21] The movement's father figure was Robert Blatchford, whose gifted socialistic writings drew in thousands of converts despite some distasteful jingoism and military-mindedness.

The National Clarion Cycling Club was officially founded at a rally of 200 Northern cyclists at Ashbourne, an event which so alarmed local residents that, according to the Clarion cyclist's own magazine, it was hardly safe for a Clarion cyclist to ride through the town a year later, so bitter was the feeling against the club.[22] Two years later there were seventy-

86 A cartoon from the radical *Clarion* newspaper.

seven local Clarion cycling clubs and by 1909 there were 230, almost all in the North of England. Clarion fellowship was reinforced by the club badge, the wearing of red caps (by some cycling clubs) and by a rag bag of little rituals such as the shout of 'Boots!' on spying a fellow Clarionette cycling, the latter being required to respond by shouting 'Spurs!', indicating that he or she had no need of assistance. This exchange, an example of what became known as 'Clarionese', originated from a barrack-room story published by Blatchford. Pleasure was integrated with politics. Club runs to country villages were opportunities to distribute socialist literature to the inhabitants. Clarion cyclists, or 'Knights of the Whirring Wheel' as they called themselves in a club song, helped out when their region was visited by Clarion Vans, horse-drawn carriages which brought literature and orators to the countryside. Like their German counterparts they used their bicycles for electioneering: a phenomenon which was not specifically socialist. In the week before the 1895 general election 300 supporters of the Conservative candidate in stoutly middle-class Brixton cycled in parade around the area each evening, with their machines festooned with election literature. The candidate was elected.[23] In the same elections Ben Tillett, the dockers' leader, and an enthusiastic cyclist, failed to be elected to West Bradford despite all the cycling efforts of the Bradford Clarionettes.

It is unlikely that many of the early Clarionettes were manual workers. The tone and advertising in their magazine, *The King of the Road*, suggests a readership with incomes beyond those of the labourer or even the semi-skilled. The movement did have a few middle-class members and wealthy supporters, such as Christabel and Sylvia Pankhurst, but its ethos remained working-class.

Both the Clarion Fellowship and the Cycling Club were sympathetic to women. Cycling Club photographs in a 1903 events programme show about a third of the club members to be women. Blatchford himself was later to write: 'Beneficial as women's suffrage has been I should place it second to the pneumatic tyre in the general life of our working people. Yes: I mean it. It is good that men and women should not live apart. When they are deprived of each other's society they deteriorate.'[24]

A more politically engaged body of Clarion cyclists were the Clarion Scouts, whose name and use of military ranks were very probably a reflection of Blatchford's military background. They were mostly adults and had no connection with Baden-Powell's scouts. Their song reveals something of their methods:

> ... Down to the haunts of the parson and the squire
> Putting opponents to rout;
> Bestriding his steed with a pneumatic tyre,
> Through village and hamlet, thro' mud and thro' mire

Rideth the Clarion Scout.
Nailing down lies and disposing of fables,
Improving the landscape by sticking up labels . . .[25]

In the United States the Labour Party organised a Socialist Wheelmen's Club in early 1898. It had a uniform of light brown jacket, blue sweater and tie, and a cap of socialist red. Shortly after the club's foundation the members rode from Boston to New York distributing their literature on the way.[26]

While the politicised worker-cyclists of the world sought active forms of leisure the masses had taken to cycling as a spectator sport. Professional cyclists had become public performers, and their working lives were hedged in by the commercial interests of events promoters, tracks owners, cycle manufacturers and newspaper proprietors. Ethical standards were perceived to have fallen considerably by the turn of the century. In March 1898 the Australian *Bulletin* published a cartoon showing two racing cyclists standing by a bar counter: 'What tyres were you wearing when you won the Gatemoney Handicap?' asked one. 'Dunno', said his friend, 'I haven't been paid yet!' In the United States track racing reached new depths of corruption and foul play once the LAW had renounced control. Events were plagued by intimidation, pushing and the 'pocketing' of opponents, whereby riders penned in a competitor while their teammate slipped past. There was one reported case of a rider caught in the act of being secretly towed by his pacing team by means of a length of piano wire which he held in his teeth. Professional track racing never reached mass popularity in Britain in the 1890s, and towards the end of that period it seemed to lose its appeal in those countries, especially France and the United States, where it had found favour. New records were becoming harder to beat, and new sensations harder for promoters to find. There is no convincing evidence that falling ethical standards were the cause of customers' dissatisfaction. In France, where heavy investment in velodromes had to be recouped, track owners responded to falling gates by introducing elements of the circus and the music hall. Scantily-dressed actresses, cycling acrobats, negro minstrels and performing animals were all brought in, but to no avail.

Some of the more degrading but most popular events in professional cycling were the six-day races of the 1890s. They were a revival of the British races of the late 1870s and early 1880s. The American versions were characterised by heavy betting, bad language and pickpocketing. Fans drifted in and out during the daytime, numbers swelled in the evenings, and fell off again after midnight. To encourage impromptu sprints some fans offered inducements by waving dollar bills from the trackside, as a dog might be offered a bone. In the centre of the Madison Square Gardens track were the riders' tents, cots and cooking stoves. There was music from a bandstand

and announcements from a giant megaphone mounted on a tripod. Competitors normally rode twenty hours per day and needed to complete 1350 miles to qualify for prize money. They were lucrative events and attracted top riders from Europe. There were reports of 'brain aberrations' among six-day cyclists. Some, apparently, imagined that their machines were glued to the spot, or that spectators were pelting them with stones. Sometimes they dismounted, stood still and gaped cluelessly. After winning the 1897 Madison Square Gardens event the American Charlie Miller complained of swollen ankles and a great sensitivity to cigar smoke, to dust rising from between the floorboards, and to the nailheads in the planking which jarred him 'fearfully'. Conditions began to cause public concern and the States of New York and Illinois limited riding time to twelve hours out of twenty-four. This and other legislation led promotors to bring in six-day team events and the competitions managed to retain some popularity till well into the Great Depression.[27]

87 Edwardian cyclists enjoyed the British countryside during a period which many consider to have been its best. Much of traditional rural life remained; the landscape had not yet been monotonised by large-scale farming and forestry, the roads were relatively good but not busy, and the countryside lay close by most towns in the days before suburban growth.

88 The Brunswick Cycling Club of Newcastle making whoopee at their temporary headquarters at the annual North East Cyclists' Meet at Barnard Castle in 1902. Clubs took over and decorated local hotels for the weekend. They performed sketches in the castle grounds and took part in a fancy dress procession through the town.

There is evidence that the general level of cycling activity in Britain rose after the demise of the Society boom. At Easter 1898, for example, 50,000 cyclists were dispatched by train from Waterloo in a single week, a large increase over the previous year's figures. Many of the middle and upper middle classes continued to cycle-tour. The diaries of A. C. Benson, son of an archbishop and a leading figure in the Edwardian literary establishment, describe how he used his bicycle to discover the quiet delights of rural England. He found it fast enough to cover the ground but slow enough to allow his photographic or (as he put it) 'somewhat microscopic' eye to notice little incidents and telling details. Benson paid tribute to his bicycle by composing, in the Summer of 1902, an addition to St Francis' *Hymn to the Sun*:

> Praised be thou, O my Lord, of our brother the *bicycle*,
> Who holdeth his breath when he runneth,
> And is very swift and cheerful and unwearied, and silent.
> He beareth us hither and thither very patiently,
> And when he is sick he doth not complain.[28]

89 Gunpowder-filled anti-dog pellets were marketed in the Netherlands and Germany, and a handlebar-grip revolver for the purpose was for sale in the Netherlands. In the United States there was the Dog-Scare, a patent ammonia squirter. There were other methods: some cyclists threw pepper, or showered dogs with stones kept handy in a pocket.

Less leisured newcomers to cycling enjoyed their Sunday runs and saved omnibus fares during the working week. The CTC lost 42,000 members between 1899 and 1910. The loss may have been partly due to the new interest in petrol engines as opposed to pedals, but is more likely to reflect the fact that few of the new cyclists had time for extensive touring. The very personal pleasures and benefits experienced by the new cyclists cannot be measured in the manner of club membership or bicycle production figures: Irene Pickering remembers cycle rides in the Ripon area around 1904:

> Dad was very fond of cycling; he used to go cycling in his dinner hour and half hour very often with Stan Todd and John King. Later when we were little tots during his rides he would sometimes, during closing time, put me on a cushion on the crossbar and I held onto the handlebars and Reg sat behind and held onto Dad and he cycled all around, in the villages and the moors. I loved the moors and am still thrilled when I hear the song of the curlew.[29]

The automobile, whose development had so long been postponed in Britain by public hostility and restrictive legislation, had its speed limit raised from 4 m.p.h. to 12 m.p.h. in 1896. This induced the Chief Constable of Surrey, a man well known for his anti-motorist sentiments, to buy 125

Singer bicycles so that specially trained policemen might overtake and apprehend motorists who broke the new speed limit. The extended limit made the automobile more attractive to those of the moneyed classes who sought an item of conspicuous consumption to replace the increasingly 'over-available' bicycle. In 1903 the speed limit was raised to 20 m.p.h., and by 1904 there were 24,201 private motor cars on the roads, the number increasing five-fold in the ensuing ten years. Royal patronage was readily forthcoming and in 1906 King Edward was proud to have exceeded 60 m.p.h. on the Brighton Road (three times the speed limit). The Automobile Association was founded in 1897 and its first patrols consisted of

90 Mikael Pedersen and his invention, the hammock-saddled Dursley Pedersen bicycle, manufactured in Dursley, Gloucestershire. It became popular at the turn of the century among those who could afford it. It was light, strong enough and distinguishing, but suffered from being introduced at the tail-end of the boom, and from its inventor's failings as a businessman. The machine shown is a military folding version which, along with other accessories he had invented, Pedersen was trying (unsuccessfully) to sell to the British army, then engaged in the Boer War. His attire is probably the one he wore on a 112 mile publicity ride.

eight cyclists, part of whose job it was to warn members of police speed traps. The arrival of the motor car re-established private transport as a proving ground for class privilege and, to some extent, for male prerogative. In *Motors and Motor Driving* (1906) Lord Northcliffe wrote, with telling superciliousness: 'Lady cyclists were formerly a great danger, as they were apt, when a motor car was heard approaching them from behind, to fall off their machines, apparently in terror; but this distressing spectacle is now comparatively rare.'

From the developmental point of view early motor vehicles showed a substantial inheritance of bicycle technology and, indeed, were almost all made by cycle companies. Many cyclists accepted motor vehicles as representing no more than a welcome and logical extension of cycle technology and leisure patterns. Others resented the invasive noise of the petrol engine and the road dust thrown up. In the words of one of H. G. Wells's characters, 'The world had thrown up a new type of gentleman altogether, a gentleman of most ungentlemanly energy, a gentleman in dusty oilskins and motor goggles and a wonderful cap, a stink-making gentleman, a swift, high-class badger, who fled perpetually along high roads from the dust and stink he perpetually made.' (*The War in the Air*, 1908) The passage refers to motor-cycles, of which there were 125,000 by 1914 and it may have been that their existence helped smudge the class distinctions which increasingly attached to cycles on the one hand and motor cars on the other. The Clarion Fellowship formed a motor-cycle club in 1913 and the *CTC Gazette* carried regular Motor Cycling Notes.

Faced by falling membership, most of the major continental cycle-touring organisations began to recruit and represent motorists. The CTC, whose secretary, Shipton, was an enthusiastic motor man, tried to follow suit. It was criticised by members for underhand politicking and for failing to publish dissenting letters in its *Gazette*. The cause was taken up by *Cycling* magazine, which gave a platform for dissidents and issued a poster saying 'CTC-ites, Save your Club!' Ironically, *Cycling* was itself giving increased coverage to motorised matters at this time. The CTC went to court in 1906, needing judicial permission to change its articles of association, but the judge disallowed the proposal, ruling that the club could not protect cyclists and at the same time espouse the very people who were a danger to them.[30] The decision showed remarkable insight.

7
CYCLING BETWEEN THE WARS

Wheels for almost Everyone

THROUGHOUT THE 1880s and 1890s armchair tacticians had debated the future role of the bicycle in warfare, but high expectations were not fulfilled in the Boer War of 1899 to 1902. On war being declared the Boers commandeered the bicycles of Johannesburg and even built a few rail-bicycles from multicycles arranged in parallel. The British army brought BSA folding bicycles which, according to General Bull, were useful for scouting: 'The bicycle has proved very useful during the present war. The rider is less conspicuous than he would be on a horse, though of course he has to risk punctures and gears going out of order.' Bicycles were probably less useful than the General cared to say, and many were abandoned by infantrymen. There is no evidence of the use of a bicycle designed for war correspondents which had been described in the *Regiment* magazine of the 24 October 1896: 'Upon the handlebar is to be attached a typewriter on which the operator will record all his impressions of the battle surging around him.' By the time of the First World War, motor as well as cycle technology were available to the military, and motor-cycles were widely used. In the early days of the conflict bicyclist battalions in the British and French armies worked in conjunction with cavalry regiments, but the German cavalry had been less willing to be associated with cycling soldiers. Once warfare had become static cyclists were used as dispatch-riders and to provide occasional rapid reinforcement.

The war over, many returning British officers spent their gratuities on motor cars. The automobile industry, which had been retarded by the war, moved towards mass-production in the post-war years. By 1922 an Austin Seven or an imported Ford Model T cost around £175, and a standard bicycle around £5. Whereas the motor car was to offer endless lucrative possibilities for stylistic embellishment and mechanical complication, the bicycle had reached a plateau of development before the Great War, and was to remain little changed till the late 1920s. The freewheel mechanism had become generally available, solving the problem of bringing the pedal crank up to '11 o'clock' when starting off, and making coasting easier and safer. The Sturmey-Archer three-speed gear came as a boon to many: Raleigh were producing 100,000 gear units a year by 1913. Rim brakes replaced 'spoon' brakes, which had operated ineffectively onto the tyre tread, and all-weather hub brakes became available. Oil lamps had been supplemented in the late 1890s by brighter and slightly more manageable acetylene lamps which lit up when water from a 'reservoir' dripped onto calcium carbide to produce an acetylene gas. These lamps were superseded during the 1930s by dynamo and battery systems.

The cycle factories of Europe produced roadsters in their millions between the wars but a handful of British manufacturers, including Lea-Francis and Beeston-Humber, produced machines of outstanding quality. The bicycle with the very highest reputation was Marston and Co.'s Golden Sunbeam, with its integral oil-bath chaincase, durable 'all-weather' finish and real gold leaf. More humble bicycles were produced by small cycle businesses which made their own frames and added readily available standardised parts. This kind of machine was usually sold to a local clientele, perhaps restricted to the maker's own town. However, the great majority of British cycles were produced by large and established firms such as BSA, Rudge-Whitworth, Raleigh, Triumph, Swift and Royal Enfield. In 1926 the Raleigh factory was claimed to be the most self-contained in the world. It produced its own gas and electricity and drew water from its own wells. It was a huge metropolis of machinery turning out 3000 cycles per week.[1] The larger cycle manufacturers re-established lost export markets by supplying sturdy and serviceable machines and by improved, imaginative commercial practices. A bizarre example of the extent of their cross-cultural marketing was revealed in a photograph, published in *Cycling* (4 Feb. 1927), of a cycle agent's window display in Reval, Estonia, showing a Red Indian shooting off an arrow as he rode a Royal Enfield.

In the heady days of 1895 an advertisement for the Rudge-Whitworth Co. had urged readers to 'follow the fashion set by Royalty, the Aristocracy and Society'. By the 1920s manufacturers were tapping very different aspirations. A glossy Raleigh pamphlet of 1923 asked:

Is your life spent among whirring machinery, in adding up columns of figures, in attending to the wants of often fractious customers? Don't you sometimes long to get away from it all? Away from the streets of serried houses ... only a few miles away is a different land, where the white road runs between the bluebell-covered banks crowned by hedges from which the pink and white wild rose peeps a shy welcome.

Sheltering amongst the trees you see the spire of the village church—beyond it that quaint old thatched cottage where the good wife serves fresh eggs and ham fried 'to a turn' on a table of rural spotlessness, for everything is so *clean* in the country ... Rosy health and a clear brain is what Raleigh gives you ...[2]

91 A 1929 line drawing by Frank Patterson, the celebrated artist of leisure cycling. His art was idyllic in tone, and complemented the heady prose of those cycle adverts which stressed not so much the merits of a given bicycle, but rather the kinds of places it would allow one to escape to.

Thus manufacturers echoed the earlier exhortations of the Clarion movement and, around 1925, began making lightweight touring bicycles for a widening market, using technology which had previously been confined to competitive cycling. The fresh-air philosophy of cycling was also encouraged by a fall in the standard number of working hours—from fifty-three hours per week in 1910 to forty-eight hours in the 1930s—and by an increase in holiday-with-pay arrangements, although about ten million workers were denied such benefits till legislation of 1938 was implemented after the war.

The upsurge in walking, climbing, cycling and camping was at its most potent between 1929 and 1933, years of economic slump and uncertainty. The *News Chronicle*'s *Cycling and Open Road Annual* of 1932, a booklet for 'wayfarers of the wheel and shoe', noted that the previous year had seen 'a boom in open-air life. Hundreds of thousands of people took to the road for the first time.' The Great Outdoors was cheap, reviving and relatively close. In *English Journey* (1934) J. B. Priestley passed judgement on the outdoor people he overtook in the course of a Sunday morning car journey into the hills around Bradford:

Before we used to set out in twos and threes, in ordinary walking clothes, for our Sunday tramps. Now they were in gangs of either hikers or bikers, twenty or thirty of them together and all dressed for their respective parts. They almost looked German. We passed the hikers very early on our journey, so I cannot say much about them, except to doubt whether this organised, semi-military, semi-athletic style of exploring the countryside is an improvement upon our old casual rambling method. These youngsters looked too much as if they were consciously taking exercise: they suggested the spirit of the lesser and priggish Wordsworth rather than the old magician who had inspired us. We saw a good deal of the cyclists, however, passing troups of them all along the road up to Grassington; and I remember wondering exactly what pleasure they were getting from the surrounding country, as they never seemed to lift their heads from the handlebars, but went grimly on like racing cyclists. They might just as well, I thought, be going round and round the city. But perhaps they call an occasional halt, and then take in all the beauty with a deep breath. There was plenty to take, too, that morning.[3]

The 'Outdoors' movement corresponded to a longer-established outdoor tradition in Germany, which was later to become Nazified as the 'Strength through Joy' movement. Long before Nazification the German example led to the establishment of the Youth Hostels Association in Britain in 1930. Even German vocabulary was used: 'Half the joy of Britain's rising wanderlust is due to the smile of the Lady Freedom', proclaimed the previously mentioned *Cycling and Open Road Annual*.

In 1934 H. G. Wells contrasted the cycling boom of the 1890s with the inter-war revival: 'The cyclist had a lordliness', he wrote, 'a sense of masterful adventure that has gone from him now.'[4] That the easy-going, country-loving, long-shorted touring cyclist lacked a certain lordliness may well have been true, but Wells's judgement ignores the exhilaration and fulfilment which cycling brought to the ordinary and anonymous escapees from factories, shops and offices. For many of them the bicycle was as exciting a novelty as it had been for the socially advantaged of the 1890s. Mrs I. Cattaneo, who was a process worker at Rowntrees chocolate factory, York, in the 1930s, later recalled her Clarion cycling experiences:

The cycling club was the highlight of my life. I had never known holidays or been anywhere until we got this bike and went all over and had such good fun and such nice company ... I didn't want money then 'cos I had this bike. We would pack up on a Sunday and we would call anywhere at these cafés, and they would give you as much tea as you wanted to drink for fourpence ... I loved that cycle and I loved every Sunday.[5]

The Clarion movement between the wars had lost much of its pre-1914 political flavour, although attitudes varied from club to club. Mrs Cattaneo in York was unaware of any political leanings whatsoever in the club. The National Clarion Cycling Club sent competitors to a succession of international Workers' Olympiades from 1925 to the late 1930s, and organised relay rides to raise money for the Republican cause in Spain. But it was as a workers' leisure organisation that the movement really thrived, and the Clarion Cycling Club's membership rose to 7000 in 1936. Members centred much of their activity on the movement's chain of 'club-houses', which preceded official youth hostels by at least fifteen years.

The cause of rational dress for women made very slow headway. Everyday clothing remained restrictive for the everyday woman cyclist, but sport-oriented women began riding in trousers or short skirts. This was still controversial enough in 1920 to draw an avalanche of correspondence

92 The Warrington Cycling Club in about 1919. There is no attempt to strike the kind of dignified pose which so characterised cycle club photographs before the turn of the century.

93 Annie Sharp, the Marnhull (Dorset) postwoman in 1914.

in *Cycling* (10, 17, 24 June). One reader felt that 'our cycling girls' did well to wear rationals in many circumstances but he knew 'scores of men who feel ... that when they meet "Miss Right" she will not be so attired'. Most letters were more reasonable: 'I am the vice-captain of a large club where a score or more rationals are now in use ... they give the club every satisfaction, and we travel much faster than the average mixed club.' Shared leisure activities were thawing the relationships between the sexes, on the dance-floors as much as on the roads. At the same time there was an increase in cycling activities principally for women. During the First World War, for example, the women CTC members of London initiated an annual Lady Cyclists' Rally. The usual route was from Ditton to Wisley Woods for a picnic, and then to the 'tea-place' at Hampton Court. Many women formed their own cycling clubs. The Rosslyn Ladies' Cycling Club was formed in the East of London in the early 1920s, and promoted the first ladies' twelve hour race. In 1934 five working girls from Newcastle upon Tyne who enjoyed cycling together formed the Elite Ladies' Cycling Club. (The name derived from a chance remark and implies no snobbishness.) Members went on eleven to twelve mile day rides as well as youth hostel tours. They regularly covered a hundred miles in a day and wore shirts, shorts, alpaca jackets and knee-length stockings, although the effect was mitigated when they took out their knitting at rest stops, for which they were nicknamed the 'Guillotine Ladies'. The women sometimes took part in race events and wore black tights for the purpose. After a Sunday's cycling activities the club met up with other returning clubs at Ponteland, a village outside Newcastle, where, according to one member, 'We used to walk up and down and the lads used to look at us, but it never went any further than that!' The Elite Ladies still meet regularly, but gave up cycling around 1970 'when little boys started shouting that the over-sixties were on the loose again'.[6]

The inter-war activities of a large London club, the Norwood Paragons, have been described by Mr Ken Hounsel.[7] He joined the club on acquiring his first bicycle at the age of sixteen, having previously hired bicycles for a penny per hour from a private house from which a fleet of thirty to forty machines were operated. He took part in club road events held on a Sunday morning between six and seven o'clock, so as to avoid traffic, and recalls that around 1929 the club used to cycle down country lanes to Brands Hatch where they trained on what was then a grass-track. Each Easter they went to the tarmac track at Herne Hill to watch the professionals, and sometimes a club member would don a helmet and compete. Many members went on training rides of forty miles or so after work. There was also a rich social life in the evenings, provided by the network of London cycling clubs, whose club-houses could be visited during the week and whose tea dances could be enjoyed at weekends.

94 A Cyclists' Touring Club road event in the 1920s, passing through Newcastle upon Tyne. It was important to approach tramlines at a safe angle, since a fall was almost inevitable if a wheel got stuck in a groove. Another danger were the wood sets laid around the tramlines. They collected oil and grease, and were slippery in the wet.

A major social centre for clubmen was often their adopted cycle shop, which usually offered a discount. Arnold Elsegood, a dealer and cycle-maker in York, recalls clubmen spending hours chatting around his brazing hearth as he worked. He was given very particular frame-making commissions by members of the club, to which he himself belonged. The growing demand for high-performance cycles was met by highly skilled craftsmen whose down-to-earth names—Grubb, Butler, Quinn, Briggs, Bates—were eloquent enough as guarantees of quality. The clubman–frame-builder relationship is little changed today. By the 1930s great advances had been made in frame tube technology and specialists were making tighter-angled frames which gave a short wheelbase and a correspondingly responsive ride. Most parts and accessories were made of British steel: alloy parts were increasingly available but were expensive. In the mid-1930s Reg Harris, the future cycling star, paid £1 for a pair of alloy handlebars and stem while earning 5p per hour in a manual job. Most serious cyclists were disdainful of the freewheel mechanism and preferred to ride fixed-wheel. By the late 1930s, however, the mechanically exposed derailleur gear system had become popular: the moving chain could be thrown from one rear cog onto one of a number of parallel cogs of different sizes, all enclosing a freewheel mechanism.

Although time trialling was a favourite clubman's activity, many went in for track racing, where the professional–amateur distinction was increasingly smudged. Some such events were nominally NCU-governed and others were 'illegal'. Prizes generally consisted of household goods, and some competitors rode for specific items: a second prize might be more welcome than a first. Prizes such as grandfather clocks, tables and armchairs were often unwelcome since they could not be carried home on a bicycle, but it was usually possible to exchange prizes for cash one way or another. Some called it shamateurism, others realism.

Very distant cousins of the clubmen's speed machines were the high street tradesmen's delivery cycles. 'To Grocers, Confectioners, Fishmongers,

95 'Hats off to the Errand Boy' was the title of the *Cycling* article in which this collage of London carrier cyclists appeared in 1939.

96 In 1939 Peters' Carrier Cycles of Wimbledon not only manufactured delivery bicycles but also maintained service contracts on several thousand machines, for which they ran a fleet of twenty Royal Enfield motor-cycle combinations. Their activities reached as far north as Carlisle.

Poulterers, Butchers and other dealers in comestibles', advertised a manufacturer, 'the carrier cycle is by far and away the cheapest method of distribution ... (it) makes a horse and cart unnecessary, saves the cost of fodder (and) enables you to employ a messenger boy instead of paying a vanman's wages.' Carrier cycles were built solid enough to survive a succession of careless and often diminutive errand boys. Since punctures could mean a loss of income to the tradesmen, non-pneumatic 'cushion' tyres were fitted to many machines, including Thomas Wall's fleet of Stop-Me-and-Buy-One ice cream tricycles, of which he had 4000 in London in 1939.[8] A carrier cycle's weight was not of prime concern to makers or buyers. Box tricycles could weigh up to a hundredweight and, having good stress distribution and innate stability, could carry up to two and a half hundredweight, although this was merely a manufacturer's standard recommended maximum. For some boys the job offered an otherwise unobtainable opportunity to cycle; for others it was a daily drudge. It was an all-year activity, and downpours often called for improvisations such as a sack slung round the shoulders or brown paper wrapped round the legs. There were complaints of some boys reading penny dreadfuls as they trundled along, and some let their friends climb aboard. Sainsbury's boys, on the other hand, were a breed apart in their smart red-trim uniforms, as were the Post Office telegraph boys in their blue uniforms with red caps. In 1938 there were 1000 telegraph boys in London and 7000 in the country as a whole. The delivery of ordered goods was not the only role of the carrier cycle. In London, and probably elsewhere, they were used by beer merchants, window-cleaners, knife-grinders, bill posters, chimney sweeps, muffin and crumpet sellers, and purveyors of cat-food. They were used to transport newspapers from the presses to the shops, and for milk deliveries: a Raleigh advertisement encouraged dairymen to 'imagine the additional ground that could be covered by the roundsman's boy with the aid of this carrier'. There was even a tricycle fish and chip shop, manufactured by Frank Ford Ltd. of Halifax in the late 1930s, which used burners fired by paraffin.

Carrier cycles became common throughout Western Europe. As early as 1902 a doctor in Germany wrote, with some justification, of the health hazards they could bring. He urged that no one under the age of twenty should be allowed on a carrier tricycle and that the maximum load should be no more than 30 kg. (66 lb). Employers should be made to provide appropriate clothing, as well as a changing room. Smoking whilst cycling should be forbidden, and a maximum speed of eight and a half kilometres per hour should be imposed.[9]

Tandems achieved a new popularity in the 1930s. Most were plain and heavy, despite names such as 'Stenton Glider' and 'Sun Wasp'. Couples had no need to give up cycling when their children arrived. They could carry them on 'Take-a-Chum' childseats, in side-cars or, more rarely, in trailers.

Bicycles became general utility vehicles. They crowded the racks outside factories and, at lunchtimes and the ends of shifts, sudden bell-ringing torrents of cloth-capped workers came cycling out of factory gates. There

97 A GPO basket carrier tricycle in 1934.

98 The *triporteurs* of Paris took part in an annual race through the city.

were, of course, other forms of transport for non-car owners. The Edwardian Era had seen a great expansion in urban tramway systems, and the rail network linked up far-flung constellations of villages and market towns. Rail travel increased three-fold between the wars. The beginnings of motorised public transport were described by Paul Evett, who cycled extensively from employment to employment before the First World War: 'Motors were just being introduced, motor buses were few and were always breaking down and temporarily abandoned by the road-side, to be jeered at by us who cycled. Motor coaches had not been thought of.'[10] But after the war it was the motor coach or char-a-banc outing which offered a sociable alternative to the bicycle as a vehicle for the pursuit of leisure. Char-a-bancs could, unlike trains, pick up passengers at their own street corners and, unlike bicycles, allowed young and old, fit and feeble to travel in each other's company. The char-a-banc outing, with its rituals and its opportunities for social intercourse, was a major emancipation for millions. It was not without critics: 'Wild motor which art crashing everywhere,/Killing pedestrian pleasure, hear, O hear! ...', wrote John Betjeman in 1921 at the age of fifteen.

The bicycle was to appear repeatedly in Betjeman's poetry: leaning against a tennis court hedge, propped against a suburban kerb, or bearing along the clean-limbed athletic women who so enraptured him. He used cycle brand names, like road names, to help evoke the spirit of a calm yet vital England, and of an uncomplicated, physical lifestyle which was vanishing before the 'wild motors ... crashing everywhere' and similar manifestations of an increasingly souped-up culture. 'Take me, my Centaur bike, down Linton Road', he wrote, describing a ride which was to take him speeding down an allotment path to a meadow where:

> ... with the Sturmey-Archer three-speed gear
> Safely in bottom, resting from the race
> We pedalled round the new-mown meadow grass
> By Marston Ferry with its punt and chain.[11]

Perhaps inevitably, the bicycle lost status at the very time of its widest use. Its exclusivity was long since gone: even young boys (not so much girls) were to be seen riding to school or delivering newspapers on glittering Royal Enfields. There had been a cycling column in the *Boys' Own Paper* as far back as the 1880s and publications such as the *Captain*, 'a magazine for boys and "old boys"', carried regular cycling columns. The *Captain* answered correspondents' (unpublished) questions with replies such as 'You would find the Bowden Brake a capital adjunct', and with dire warnings against courses of action which we can only guess at. The columnist gave advice on 'the duties of citizenship' and warned that any cyclist

99 Newquay Sands, August 1923. Bicycle hire as a seaside recreational activity had begun in the 1890s and was still possible at some resorts after the First World War, despite the damaging effect of salt on steel.

overtaking another on the inside was 'guilty of manners which I would describe as simply vile. Should any of my readers have been thoughtlessly guilty of this practice, I trust they will think the better of it in future.'[12] Between the wars *Cycling* occasionally published approving articles on the joys of cycling for the young, accompanied by photographs of boys in school caps, gaberdines and knee-length socks stopped by the roadside studying a map. Cycling was integrated into Boy Scouts' activities. Jamborees featured cycling demonstrations, one of which involved the carrying of a stretcher by four cyclists, each having fastened one of its handles to his machine.

Losing out to the Motoring Few

The figures for deaths and injuries among cyclists rose to a peak between 1934 and 1941, at which time there were about 9 million regular cyclists and

100 Sussex CTC members at an event at Eastbourne, probably in the late 1930s.

2½ million regular drivers. In 1936 there were 1496 cyclists killed and 71,193 injured on British roads, the total of the two 1936 figures being two and a half times what it had been just eight years before. Of road casualties in 1936, 31 per cent were cyclists.[13] (The figures for 1984 are: 345 cyclists killed and 30,270 injured, being 10.4 per cent of all road casualties. The lower figures are partly due to the lower number of cyclists for modern motorists to hit.) Motorists were a danger to themselves as well as to cyclists. So high was the accident rate that in about 1926 the St John's Ambulance Brigade sent intrepid cycling first-aid patrols along certain of the main roads around London. The government's attitude to what cycling magazines justifiably called 'the carnage on the roads' was *laissez-faire*. The police were frustrated by lack of legislation. On the 10 March 1937 *Cycling* reported an outburst from the Chief Constable of Nottinghamshire at a road safety conference: 'There is only one fit and proper treatment for road hogs. That is the cat.' Another policeman at the same conference demanded a 20 m.p.h. speed limit in built-up areas. Viscountess Astor had an alternative solution to the problem of motoring in towns. Speaking in Parliament on the 4 July 1934 she suggested that 'some system could be devised to prohibit cycling in very crowded areas'.[14]

In its editorial of the 10 March 1934 *Cycling* addressed the politics of the situation. It stated that Mr Hore-Belisha, the Minister of Transport, must choose between the 'lesser important' enmity of the cyclists and the formidable opposition of the whole motoring community, which, financially and industrially, is now bound up with the life of the nation ... He is anti-cyclist because he caters primarily for an age in which none of the leaders of public thought in transport matters are cyclists.

In the same issue a leading cycling journalist, Fitzwater Wray, quoted part of a letter he had sent to Hore-Belisha:

101 A Cyclists' Touring Club rally in the 1920s on the Portsmouth Road, South West of London (now the A3). The section of the road between the Angel Inn at Thames Ditton and the Anchor Inn at Ripley became known in the 1880s as the Blue Riband, being regarded as the best kept road in the world. Cyclists even came from abroad to ride on it. The road remained dear to cyclists until motor traffic made it unconvivial.

You are reported as having said last week that our roads are now like battlefields. That was truly said, but was it not also a confession of failure? You have tried to reduce the carnage; and we few who realise the formidable forces ranged against you, truly sympathise with you in those efforts. But you cannot abolish battlefields by notice-boards. Once again, you 'appealed to the conscience of the community'; but you cannot cure a cancer by appealing to the patient's conscience. One admits that you have not had a fair deal. If you had had the support of the Home Office that you deserved in your 30 (m.p.h.) limit, a reduction of thirty per cent in road accidents would have been your reward. You have not, and the speed limit is all but dead ... The magistracy generally has treated your efforts with contempt ... *The fixing of a governor on a gas-engine is the simplest of engineering propositions!*

Being unable or unwilling to control motorists' behaviour the government attempted to give them clear roads by building segregated paths for cyclists. The policy was half-hearted. Cycle-tracks were built alongside new roads from about 1935 but only 137 miles of track had been completed or begun within two years. Although the use of cycle-tracks was voluntary they were abhorred by cyclists' organisations who saw them as presaging an attack on the cyclist's right to use the road. The tracks were, and still are, little used, being often badly made and obstructed by parked cars, litter and broken glass. Also, they gave cyclists no protection at junctions. The government's initiative petered out and was not revived after the war.

Membership of the CTC rose by 42,000 between the wars, although the club's influence in public affairs declined. An already unsympathetic Parliament was further antagonised by the CTC's stubborn opposition to the proposal that cyclists should carry red rear lights. The club argued that the onus for avoiding an accident should always rest with the overtaking vehicle. Another argument used by the club was that if motorists expected to be able to see cyclists at night they would drive faster and would kill the many cyclists whose light would, inevitably, have gone out.[15] The government finally imposed the red rear light as a wartime measure, and the legislation was made permanent in 1945, the CTC lodging one solitary objection.

In the Netherlands and Denmark cycling was established as a cultural asset. Yet so pervasive and available were bicycles that Kurt Tucholski, a visiting German writer, was moved to write a piece entitled '1372 Bicycles', this being the number of unclaimed bicycles stored in the lost property office of the Copenhagen police. In Germany the liberating ethos of cycling was subverted by the National Socialists' strident philosophy of physicality. They organised, among other things, a Day of the German Cyclist in 1933, which included a vast cycle rally of uniformed party members in Berlin.

102 The Neckarsulm Bicycle Works was one of the largest in Germany. This advertisement, from around 1920, featured the back-pedal brake with freewheel.

103 Leroux, a competitor in the 1902 Paris–Roubaix road race, is beaten by a hill. The race took (and still takes) cyclists over the damaging cobbled country roads of Northern France, towards the Belgian border. The event has become known as 'the Hell of the North'.

National Socialism was marketed through cycle shops in the form of accessories bearing swastikas. There was even a tyre which left an imprint consisting entirely of swastikas.

In France there were an estimated 7 million cyclists by 1926, but the figure rose little until 1937 and 1938 when it reached about 9 million. This was mainly due to the introduction of the forty-hour week and paid holidays, as part of the leisure policy of Leon Blum's socialist *Front Populaire* government, elected in 1936. In the few years left before the war Parisian cyclists almost monopolised the roads as they left the city for their weekend tours of the countryside. French competitive cycling was dominated by road events. In the 1930s the cycle sport press was joined by wireless broadcasting in presenting a diet of news for passive consumption. The deeds of cycling heroes were packaged in the kind of ecstatic reportage which helped bring

L'Auto (a cycling daily despite its name) 495,000 sales on one day in June 1923. The leading exponent of effusive cycle journalism was Henri Desgrange, founder of the Tour de France. He set an early example in his reporting of the 1901 Paris–Brest–Paris race:

> There are four of them. Their legs, like giant levers, will power onwards for sixty hours; their muscles will grind up the kilometres; their broad chests will heave with the effort of the struggle; their hands will clench onto their handlebars; with their eyes they will observe each other ferociously; their backs will bend forward in unison for barbaric break-aways; their stomachs will fight against hunger, their brains against sleep. And at night a peasant waiting for them by a deserted road will see four demons passing by, and the noise of their desperate panting will freeze his heart and fill it with terror.[16]

The Tour de France owes its existence to the celebrated Dreyfus affair of the late 1890s, in which a clearly innocent Jewish army officer was convicted of spying. The issue profoundly divided French society: *le Vélo*, at that time the only cycling daily, was openly pro-Dreyfus, and criticised an anti-Dreyfus demonstration in which the paper's own principal financial supporter, Baron de Dion, a bicycle industrialist, took part. De Dion withdrew his support from *le Vélo* and founded, together with other bicycle industrialists such as Clément and Michelin, a rival daily cycling newspaper, *l'Auto-Vélo* (later renamed *l'Auto* as a result of a copyright prosecution), which appointed the effusive Henri Desgrange as editor. *Le Vélo* had privileged access to cycle club information and so Desgrange needed to launch a new initiative which would outflank his rival in the circulation battle. He founded the Tour de France in 1903. It was a magnificently imaginative invention, a form of odyssey in which the lonely heroism of unpaced riders was pitted against relentless competition and elemental nature. The Tour encompassed the territory of France, and Desgrange later claimed that it encouraged a sense of national identity, establishing *la Patrie* in clear geographic terms.

The first Tour went reasonably well, despite some attempts by mobs supporting other riders to intimidate Garin, the eventual winner. The second Tour, in 1904, was a fiasco of sabotage and violence. Some riders were handed bottles of fouled water which made them ill; one was given a soporific and crashed while drowsy. One had his shirt filled with itching powder, and another his shorts filled with emery. One rider's cycle frame had been weakened by filing, causing him to crash badly. There were regular series of punctures due to handfuls of nails being thrown onto the road. The competitors were vulnerable during night stages, and at three o'clock in the morning on a mountain pass the leaders, including Garin, were set upon by a hundred or so men wielding sticks and stones. They let their favoured cyclist through and then closed in on the rest, injuring one of them badly. Only pistol shots from a race official arriving in a car dispersed the attackers. Crowd violence, road blocks and nail scattering affected the rest of the race, despite secret starts, altered routes and heavier police protection. After the race there were allegations of conspiracy between riders, team-managers and wayside thugs, and of competitors taking illicit rides in cars and tows from motorcyclists. Four months later the first four riders were disqualified and forfeited their prizes. 'The Tour is finished', wrote Desgrange on the day after the event ended, 'and I feel that its second version will have been its last. It will have died of its own success, and of the blind passions which it unleashed.'

Yet the Tour went on. The public savoured its scandals and unpredictability, and were attracted to the riders' 'epic' struggle against human vice as well as Nature. Night stages were dispensed with and the distance covered was doubled to around 5000 kilometres, divided into more and shorter stages, before the onset of the First World War. Illicit activities continued, but to a less spectacular extent. Saboteurs had discovered a kind of nail which always fell with its point upwards, and tampering with bicycles became such a problem that riders took them into their bedrooms at night. Independent competitors complained of collusion between manufacturers' teams, and of drug-taking by individuals, even before the First World War. The availability between the wars of more refined stimulants made matters worse, and along with the full commercialisation of the Tour came the introduction of urine sampling. On one occasion a competitor who cheated by supplying someone else's urine was informed that the test had proved negative but was warned that he was pregnant. Manufacturers lavished bounteous resources on their Tour de France teams. In the early 1920s the communist-controlled newspaper *Sport-Ouvrier* maintained that specific prizes had been created so that each manufacturer could claim to have won something. Manufacturers' ambitions were getting out of hand, and in 1930 the organisers replaced manufacturers' teams with national teams for a while, and the Tour derived its income more from advertising and from localities paying to host the event, than from participating manufacturers. There was a slight ethical improvement.[17]

In the United States the story of inter-war cycling was characterised by lack of interest and a steady decline. The attention of Colonel Pope, the entrepreneurial bicycle pioneer, had turned to the manufacture of automobiles, although in 1906 his company began making private-brand bicycles for large merchandising chains. There were cycling strongholds in the major cities—New York had several cycle sport clubs with around a hundred members each at the end of the First World War. But cycling had lost out to the automobile, and to some extent to the new electric transport

104 Cycling on the Pittsburgh and Western Railway in the 1920s.

systems. In the 1930s cumbersome, fat-tyred 'balloon bombers', bulbously streamlined in imitation of motor-cycles or aeroplanes, appealed to American children: the only mass market still open to cycle manufacturers. The fortunes of cycling in America were revived by petrol shortages during the Second World War. So sudden was the demand for bicycles that in April 1942 all retail selling of cycles was 'frozen' for three months, after which limited numbers were sold on certificate to defence workers. Of 9000 cycles released in July 1942 5767 went to Douglas Corporation personnel.

In wartime Britain the petrol shortage and public transport restrictions brought cycling back into political favour. Spares were hard to come by, and anyone riding in the blackout hooded or part-masked the front light. In France the bicycle helped many city-dwellers to keep starvation at bay. They could cycle out into the countryside and, avoiding police control points, bring back farm produce and game. Some Parisian taxi drivers cut

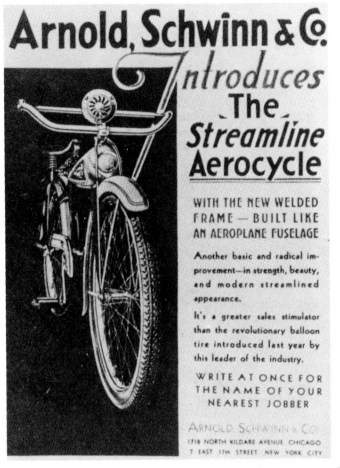

105 An American advertisement for children's cycles, from 1933. Schwinn had previously introduced bicycles whose fat tyres and frame styling had imitated motor-cycles. Such 'balloon bombers', and the subsequent Aerocycle, have become coveted collectors' items.

their cabs in half and yoked the rear sections to bicycles. At least one taxi was pulled by a team of former racing cyclists.

Wartime austerity gave cycling a short reprieve in the industrial world. The post-war peace was to lay the bicycle low.

8
CYCLING IN THE MOTOR AGE: RELAPSE AND REVIVAL

IN THE EARLY 1950s there were approximately twelve million regular cyclists in Britain, and most used their bicycles for everyday personal transport. But the British public was giving a high priority to recreation, as if in reaction to years of austerity. They filled sports stadiums and cinemas, holiday camps and seaside resorts. Many thousands of cycle-tourists continued to take quiet, private pleasure in meandering through rural lanes and villages. Such an unassuming form of recreation could not, however, attract the attention of a public which was avid for new sensations. The pursuit of leisure was becoming increasingly aligned with the acquisition of consumer goods, the most evident of which was the motor car. In the ten years after war's end the number of motor vehicles increased three-fold. Governments

106 The starting point of a cross-country reliability trial organised by the Chester branch of the Cyclists' Touring Club in 1949.

107 A resourceful CTC family in the late 40s or early 50s. Although some passenger-carrying trailers were used from the 1890s onwards it was in the 1930s that a variety of side-cars and other child-carrying devices became popular. They had become rare by the mid-1950s.

had little interest in controlling road transport and it would, in any case, have been politically inexpedient to deny working people a luxury which had for so long been a status symbol of the affluent. Although private motorists constituted only a minority of transport-users their aspirations dominated. An anonymous article in the *Police Journal* of October 1954 complained that

> A large section of the press, as well as the BBC, seem dominated by the motoring interests, and even such reputable bodies as the Chambers of Commerce, the AA and RAC, pay lip service to road safety but do not hesitate to join the barrage of opposition to any regulations ... which may affect the drivers of cars adversely.[1]

So imperative was the motoring cause that it made cyclists seem like unenterprising and insignificant social stragglers. They began to be treated as such. Whenever motoring organisations took account of cyclists or pedestrians it was by way of training them to cope with traffic rather than by offering any attempt at self-reform. From about 1949 onwards the Pedestrians' Association demanded government intervention in 'the scandal of ROSPA' (Royal Society for the Prevention of Accidents), claiming that it

163

had been created by representatives of the motoring interests and was still controlled by them. The CTC resigned from ROSPA, arguing that the latter's publicity assumed that the victims of road accidents were themselves to blame. In 1954 it was pointed out that the new president of ROSPA was the chairman of Vauxhall Motors, and that the chairman of ROSPA's road safety committee was a leading figure in the legal department of the Society of Motor Manufacturers and Traders.[2] ROSPA continues to avoid radical criticism of transport policies, concentrating on accommodating measures such as the National Cycling Proficiency Scheme, introduced in 1959.

The total number of kilometres travelled by British cyclists dropped steadily from about 23,000 million in 1952 to just under 4000 million in 1974, at which point it began to rise.[3] CTC membership fell from 40,000 before the war to 20,000 in 1969. In 1959 the Conservative Government appointed a new transport minister, Ernest Marples (of Marples Ridgeway, civil engineers and roadbuilders), who told his party conference in 1960 that 'We have to rebuild our cities. We have to come to terms with the car.' In 1967, three years after the Conservatives had lost power, Marples was to chair a colloquium at the Royal Society of Arts on the future of cycling. Having introduced himself as 'an ex-Minister of Transport who made London's traffic go twenty per cent faster in five years with a greatly increased volume', he went on, with no hint of self-reproach, to describe how such traffic flows could intimidate cyclists. He declared that he owned a bicycle himself, which he rode in France, 'but I do not use it in London any more, because, for example, if you try and go round Hyde Park Corner on a cycle you are signing your own death warrant'.[4] In 1963 Marples' 'new era in road travel' was given academic rationale by the publication of the influential Buchanan Report.[5] The failure of this report to address the problems of cyclists deepened a suspicion that the potentates of the motoring community had tacitly agreed that cycling was too dangerous to warrant encouragement, and that it were best left to die away. Labour took office in 1964, and Barbara Castle's Integrated Transport Policy gave concerned cyclists no cause to change their views.

British cycle manufacturers experienced major difficulties in the late 1950s, and a series of take-overs left two concerns dominating the market: Tube Investments and Raleigh Industries. They themselves merged in 1960, becoming TI–Raleigh, with Raleigh handling the entire cycling side. Yet cycling enjoyed a limited return to fashion in the mid to late 1960s, inspired by the appearance in 1962 of a small-wheeled bicycle designed by Alex Moulton, an independent engineer. The rigidity and discomfort of small wheels were designed away by the use of a rubber suspension system to the front and rear of the Moulton frame. It was compact, 'unisex' and, above all, novel: 'a mini-bike to go with mini-skirts and mini-cars; all part of the "Swinging 60s"'.[6] In 1959 Moulton had offered his design to Raleigh, who

164

108 Unmodernised shop-fronts, unlined roads, and a Moulton bicycle. Alex Moulton's influential invention first appeared in 1962: a mini-bike for the era of miniskirts and mini-cars.

had turned it down. He manufactured it himself and it sold well. Meanwhile Raleigh's market research was showing that conventional bicycles and cycling had an unfashionable 'cloth cap' image, and that there was a latent demand for bicycles, particularly among women and children.

The Raleigh design department was given a *marketing* specification for a 'fun means of conveyance' with a new image. The result was the RSW 16 (Raleigh Small Wheels, 16 inch), which had flaccid two-inch wide low-pressure balloon tyres to soak up the road shocks: Moulton held the patent for the in-frame suspension system. The RSW was given an expensive publicity launch in 1965: 'Promotions were tied up with Mary Quant, with cosmetics manufacturers. Celebrities of all kinds, like Lord Robens, got new bikes and were photographed on them—anything to eliminate the idea of the bike as a workhorse.'[7]

The RSW 16, and other post-Moulton small-wheelers, were, with few exceptions, triumphs of styling over quality. Yet they enabled the status-conscious to cycle without feeling compromised by appearing too athletic. They were also stable when carrying shopping, and the upright riding position gave, to women especially, the confidence to venture onto the busy post-war roads.

Competition from Raleigh harmed Moulton's sales, and his use of some defective front forks, supplied by a sub-contractor, proved damaging. In 1967 Moulton was forced to sell his cycle company to TI–Raleigh, who continued to manufacture Moultons till 1974, by which time 250,000 had been sold world-wide. Raleigh also produced a twenty-inch wheel 'shopper bike' and then a series of 'fun' bikes for children. 'What was important', wrote a Raleigh executive, 'was the underlying realisation that bicycles are consumer goods, not bits of light engineering ... A fashion industry in which kids of all ages were the consumer was the ideal solution to Raleigh's product problems. It introduced that element of product obsolescence which the industry desperately needed.'[8]

The New Cyclists

In his best-selling book, *The Greening of America* (1970), Charles Reich identified an emergent new 'consciousness' which was in revolt against the stultifying influence of a corporate consumer-culture: 'When man allows machines and the machine-state to master his consciousness, he imperils not only his inner being but also the world he inhabits and upon which he depends.' This recovery of one's self, this profoundly optimistic search for individualising experiences, gave birth to a cycling boom in a society which had come close to dismissing any form of self-propulsion as an act of eccentricity. Reich himself made no mention of bicycles in his book, citing, instead, the motor-cycle as a vehicle of liberation from the Cadillac-mentality. Yet the pioneers of new life-styles in the United States were already appreciating the bicycle as an exciting and innocent form of transport. The bicycle renaissance was stimulated by the oil crisis of the early 1970s, when cycling became, for some Americans, a patriotic means of saving the nation's oil reserves. The great majority of machines bought at this time were heavy, multi-geared imitations of racing cycles. Nevertheless their popularity blocked off Raleigh's attempt to introduce their regressive, fat-tyred RSWs to the United States. The American bicycle boom developed along recreational rather than utilitarian or specifically radical lines. It intensified in the late 1970s, boosted by the development of a strong popular interest in health and fitness. Many cyclists and joggers took to the parks, where each activity was (and still is) often allocated a separate track. The arrival of roller-skaters with no track of their own has led to some dramatic disruption of track traffic. Rodale Press, owners of the highly popular health magazine, *Prevention*, also own *Bicycling* magazine, which itself devotes considerable space to fitness and optimum performance.

By the late 1970s large numbers of lightweight cycles were being imported from specialist makers in England and France, and American makers had raised their standards to compete. Indeed, some refined their products to a degree which was inappropriate to the practical needs of their customers: consumerism in the form of ultra-lightweight titanium frames and prestigious but irrelevant micrometre precision in the making of frames. Such excesses are not uniquely American, although American attitudes to cycling may have provided the tone for the world-wide marketing techniques of multinational cycle and accessory manufacturers. Shimano, for example, developed aerodynamic tubing and equipment for racing cycles, and then tried to transfer the innovation to the leisure market, although such streamlining gives no advantage at anything less than racing speeds. The gimmick was copied by other, less reputable, manufacturers, who took to the simple expedient of squashing their tubing. Shimano's initiative was soon recognised as no more than stylistic and was a notable flop. There were, at the same time, examples of manufacturers responding well to cyclists' needs: there have been useful advances in the design, quality and range of parts and accessories such as braking systems, touring panniers and crash helmets (which are very commonly worn by American cyclists).

As the years have passed cycling in the United States has reached an assured status and a popular (but mostly middle-class) base. A 1985 survey showed that more than 75 million Americans ride bicycles and that half of the riders were over sixteen years old. Admittedly, 26 million were only occasional cyclists and 11 million cycled only once weekly on average, but the survey did imply substantial and continuing growth in all modes.[9]

The popularity of cycling has had no discernible effect on the extent or social esteem of motoring, since the two are not generally seen as alternatives. American cyclists are commonly motorists themselves: in a 1976 survey only 5.1 per cent of them reported not having an own car available. Some eight years later the first issue of *Bicycle Rider*, a luxuriously glossy magazine gave an indication of the attitudes of the anticipated readership: its front cover featured dynamic young cyclists on an elegant drive-way, with a racey sports car parked suggestively nearby.

Cyclists in American cities suffer from heavily potholed roads, unpleasant air turbulence caused by high-rise buildings, and cycle theft. To encourage commuter-cycling progressive transport planners are advocating safe cycle parking at places of work and at suburban bus and train stops, so that commuters can cycle and then ride. In certain parts of a few larger US cities cyclists are endangered by muggers,[10] who steal their bicycles, causing more cycle-commuters to travel in groups. At the other extreme are cycle-friendly localities such as Palo Alto, a university town in California, where legislation has been introduced for compulsory cycle-stands at all parking lots, for certain banks and fast food outlets to provide 'drive-in' facilities for cyclists, for 'bicycle boulevards' and for traffic signals sensitive to bicycles. Public employees receive a mileage allowance for cycling to work, and all government offices, along with restaurants and bars over a certain size, must have showers for cyclists' use.

The superior speed of a bicycle in urban areas has encouraged the growth of cycle messenger businesses. The freestyle road behaviour of some messengers and of some other urban cyclists, is causing concern, especially to pedestrians. Some New York cyclists have become accustomed to ignoring traffic lights, pedestrian crossings and no entry signs: partly as a survival strategy. The owner of one cycle messenger business said: 'It's murder out there. I have to put video games in the office to calm messengers down at the end of the day.'[11]

The Californian epicentre of the American cycling boom has generated a succession of innovations in cycling and transmitted them abroad. In 1976 Dr Chester Kyle formed the International Human-Powered Vehicle Association, which encouraged the development of a radical new generation of streamlined and recumbent cycles. These sleek machines are mostly bicycles and tricycles in which one or more riders sit back in an almost supine position so that the pedal resistance force is taken by the back of the seat. On

109 A race of motley human-powered vehicles. In speed record attempts, and under many other circumstances, HPVs can out-perform racing cycles. HPV racing is a fast growing and visually exciting sport.

some versions the rider pedals lying face-down. Some cycles are open, to prevent the occupant from overheating and to avoid the effects of unbalancing side-winds. Others are enclosed in streamlining plastic or fibreglass shells. In speed record attempts, and under many other circumstances, HPVs can out-perform conventional racing cycles and have long since been excluded from recognition by the Union Cycliste Internationale, the principal governing body for cycle sport. This ban had previously frustrated experiments in alternative cycle design in the 1930s, especially in France. The UCI's well-meaning restrictions, intended to isolate the individual competitor's performance from the distortions of technology, are almost comic in their complexity: 'The distance from the vertical plane of the saddle peak to that of the bracket axle must not exceed 4¾ inches ...'

Restrictions have been eased a little in recent years due to the instant nature of new design and technology. The International Human-Powered Vehicle Association, having few restrictions, has opened up the designers' horizons. Some design teams are university based, with technology such as vacuum plastics at their disposal; others are 'garden-shed' inventors who could trace their lineage back to the independent amateur velocipede mechanics of the early nineteenth century. The Association holds annual HPV racing and record events in the United States and elsewhere. These events usually contain categories for vehicles which perform on water and in the air. Some HPV enthusiasts claim that cycles developed from the present varieties of track HPVs (which they call Phase Three cycles) will eventually become as common on the streets as the ordinary (so-called Phase Two) bicycles of the present day. Yet HPVs, as currently conceived, have drawbacks. They perform badly uphill, they are affected by adverse weather conditions, and they can be dangerously inconspicuous in traffic. On the other hand they are reported to be a thrilling form of transport on flat country roads.[12]

Another Californian innovation is the sport of BMX (bicycle motorcross), which was not so much invented as organised into existence in the late 1970s, before quickly crossing the Atlantic. Its competition form consists of helmeted young riders speeding on strengthened, specialised bicycles around purpose-built dirt tracks which include exhilarating jumps, swoops and banked turns. The machines, the clothing and the jargon are unashamedly gaudy. Freestyle BMX display riding has also developed as a distinct sport, and is emulated by young people who perform some often impressive cycle-gymnastics in their neighbourhood streets.

A third gift from California has been the 'mountain bike', built for adult off-road cycletouring. In the mid 1970s adults on motor-cycles and youths on utility bicycles made a sport of careering down steep hillsides, and then being transported back up in a truck. When motor-cycles were banned by the authorities the men switched to utility bicycles, which they thought

110 BMX: a lively new sport from the United States, backed by a multi-million dollar industry.

would be stronger than light touring cycles. The utility cycles proved too weak and their back-pedal brakes overheated. This led to a series of design changes, by amateurs and then by professional cycle makers, which resulted in a rugged but light machine with appropriately fat tyres, fifteen or more gears, powerful 'cantilever' brakes, oversized tubing and wide handlebars: generally known as the mountain bike. High specification mountain bikes are used in competitive events and long-distance off-road touring. Mass-market mountain bikes, with basic specifications, sell to middle-aged executives who want a leisure cycle without the fuss of elaborate gearing, or even toe-clips, which might scuff smart shoes. Cheaper mountain bikes are increasingly used as commuter vehicles able to cope with urban potholes and kerbs. The number of mountain bikes sold in the USA is doubling each year, but interest is developing only slowly in Europe. There is some concern over the effects of mountain-biking on ecologically sensitive land surfaces.

The fourth spasm of American innovation has been the 'triathlon', an event concocted from a long-distance swim followed by a long-distance cycle ride and then by a half-marathon run. Triathlons are mass-participation events, replacing the simple marathon as the ultimate personal challenge for a fit individual.

The oil price rise of 1973/4 also gave a boost to a sustained bicycle revival in Europe, particularly in Northern Europe. In Britain the level of cycling rose by an estimated 300 per cent in the ten years after 1974. The revival was, as in America, the result of mainly middle-class enthusiasm, although working-class traditions of utilitarian cycling had not died out in some areas, notably Cambridgeshire, Norfolk, Humberside and York. As in the United States, the British boom has been well supplied with a wide choice of new equipment, magazines, books and commercially organised cycling holidays. Special interest clubs, such as the Tandem Club, the Tricycle Association, the Moulton Users' Club, and others which cater for imported

111 Mountain bikes are designed for rough terrain, using modern lightweight technology. Mountain bike events, usually on cross-country courses, are becoming a major sport in the US and are establishing themselves in Europe. Some enthusiasts have taken to long-distance cross-country touring. It is probable that most mountain bike riding takes place on American and Canadian city streets, especially in cities whose street maintenance has been neglected.

112 Family transport: the author and family on tandem tricycles. The machine on the left is towing an articulated, detachable Hann trailer.

113 A purpose-built child-carrying 'shopping' tricycle by the English tricycle specialist, Ken Rogers. Shopping tricycles are stable, sociable and useful work-horses. Also, considerable loads can be carried on a platform beneath the child-seats. In York there are approximately fifty in daily use.

American cycle sports, have thrived on increased membership. The Veteran-Cycle Club is the strongest association for enthusiasts of cycle history and restoration and has a wide national and international base. It had over 1000 members in early 1986. The boom has been provided with new institutions such as the annual London to Brighton Bike Ride on which over 25,000 motley riders cover fifty-six miles on a single summer Sunday. There is also National Bike Week, an annual promotion event. It is probably safe to say that the social status of cycling has improved in the last decade. It is finding its way into films and even into advertising agencies' repertoire of images. Hoardings advertise packets of Persil soap powder being carried home on a shopping bike; but a more usual image has been that of a floppy-hatted beauty in flowing white dress cycling mistily through an idyllic meadow: reminiscent of the image of women cyclists current in the High Society boom of the 1890s.

When not riding through idyllic meadows some women cyclists face the problem of sexual harassment. A correspondent to the *Daily Cyclist* wrote:

> Almost every day I receive comments because I am a woman on a bicycle ... Men save their oppressive comments for the numerous occasions when traffic noise will ensure that only you will hear what they say, or for when, after dark or on quiet streets, there is no-one else around ... Is this why most male cyclists remain blissfully unaware of what goes on?[13]

The 'new cyclists' of the 1970s and 80s have, in general, been more demonstrative and impatient than older established cyclists. They have tended to be more radical in their outlook: members of cycle campaigns, supporters of pressure groups. They have shown little interest in what they regard as the cosy world of seasoned clubmen, of plus-fours-civility. The *Daily Cyclist*, a publication of the London Cycling Campaign, features a spoof column by an irascible, narrow-minded old clubman named Backpedaller, who harks back to his days with the 'Bluebridge Wheelers'. In *Bicycle Magazine* Nigel Thomas, a cycle journalist, wrote of 'Britain's cycling establishment, stern keeper of the faith during the dark age of the Cortina, and now eager to claim its inheritance in the sun-dappled lanes of the Second Age of the bike'.[14] The 'old guard' have criticised in their turn, feeling that aggressive or flamboyant behaviour harms the status and image of cycling. And they had, after all, 'kept the faith'.

The Cyclists' Touring Club was at first slow to respond to new developments, viewing with suspicion the attitudes of campaign groups. Throughout the 1970s the Club's magazine, *Cycletouring*, exuded an air of gentle companionableness and, indeed, locally organised club-runs, rallies and social events remain valued and important aspects of the CTC's activities. Membership rose, but not in line with the boom, and the Club seemed to be insufficiently attractive to those younger cyclists who might eventually guarantee its future. In 1982 a Reform Group made itself heard, accusing the club of lethargy and undue self-satisfaction. The group soon disappeared. It may not have had broad support and the Club was, in any case, in the process of gradual change. The CTC in the 1980s has intensified its commitment to furthering cyclists' rights, shown a new vigour in dealing with government agencies, and has co-operated more closely with the transport campaigners from younger pressure groups.

The new cyclists have formed autonomous local cycling pressure groups, the largest of which has been the London Cycling Campaign, which enjoyed support from the Greater London Council prior to that body's abolition. The cycle pressure groups are kept in touch with each other by Friends of the Earth, which also publishes a quarterly *Bicycles Bulletin*, a journal for campaigners and transport planners. Friends of the Earth's recent policy has been to integrate cyclists' welfare with other transport issues, in an attempt to present a coherent range of alternatives to the existing situation. The Cycle Campaign Network, which is distinct from Friends of the Earth, meets twice a year to formulate co-ordinated approaches to other organisations and agencies.

Cycle campaigning, as practised by Friends of the Earth, the CTC and local campaign groups, involves research, report-writing, media work and the supplying of technical advice to local authorities in the absence of such advice from the Department of Transport. At national level a handful of underfunded paid workers face the comfortably financed and well-connected representatives of the road construction companies, car manufacturers, road hauliers, petrol-purveyors, motorists' associations and urban renewal industries. The cycling lobby has compensated for its lack of funds and 'establishment' connections by the use of political lobbying on an environmental platform. Although physical achievements have been limited to a few hundred miles of cycle path and converted railway line, many local authority planners and engineers are paying more attention to the cyclist in terms of traffic management.

The only sector which has benefitted financially from the cycling boom— the bicycle industry—has never engaged in the push and shove of road politics, probably in the belief that to draw attention to the dangers of cycling would suppress demand for their products.

The upsurge in cycling, just when motor traffic seemed about to clinch its monopoly, came as an inconvenience to those who govern. While perhaps wishing that the awkward phenomenon would go away, the British Government issued, in 1982, a brief Cycling Policy Statement, which gave, for the first time ever, official support for more and safer cycling. This magnanimity was subsequently narrowed down to the issue of accident reduction amongst cyclists: an abandonment of the commitment to encourage cycling,

114 A campaigning cartoon by Borin van Loon and used by Friends of the Earth, London, in the early 1980s.

and a return to the view that cycling should be treated as a problem rather than an opportunity. The Department of Transport's response to the 'problem' lay in a half-hearted experimentation in cycle lane design, with very few implementations. In their book, *The Needless Scourge*, Stephen Plowden and Mayer Hillman argue that half-hearted policies could be worse than none, since they might encourage more cycling without any commensurate protection to inexperienced new cyclists. In August 1984 the Department of Transport again shifted the emphasis of its cycling policy: from modest traffic engineering measures to a £1,000,000 publicity campaign. Posters, radio jingles and tee-shirt slogans urged cyclists and motorists to be more aware of each other. The campaign had no discernible effect on casualty levels: an outcome long ago predicted by the 1948 Social Survey, which had concluded that the public as a whole was immune to warnings about danger on the roads, and that visual propaganda had minimal effect. The safety campaign also antagonised cycling activists, who felt that blame for the 7000 cycle-related deaths and injuries each year should have been squarely attributed to the motorists. The Department of Transport's 'Share the Road' motto was echoed by Lynda Chalker, then Minister of State for Transport, who felt it was important to 'keep a balance between all road-users'.[15] Mrs Chalker carried a folding bicycle in the boot of her car, and rode it at opening ceremonies for new cycling facilities. Her superior, Nicholas Ridley, the Secretary of State for Transport, showed himself to be unequivocally a car man: 'The motorist is an individual, and he likes being a motorist

175

because he can exercise his individual freedom of choice. That is a good thing. He should not be hampered by petty rules and unnecessary restrictions on his liberty.'[16] Ridley's outlook ignores the intimidatory effect of motor traffic. A 1977 study by a Department of Transport statistician, J. R. Waldman, revealed that the existing level of cycle journeys to work in hilly, traffic-dangerous towns is 2 per cent, but would rise to 20 per cent if cycling were safer. In flat dangerous towns the level of cycling would rise from 6 per cent to 43 per cent.[17] More recent studies and experiences in Germany and the Netherlands have confirmed these findings. Although it was commissioned by the Department of Transport, the Department is reluctant to acknowledge Waldman's paper and it does not appear in the Department's official cycling bibliography.

Nicholas Ridley dismissed Plowden and Hillman's far-sighted and vitally important critique of road transport policies, *The Needless Scourge*, as a theoretical exercise by 'bicycle-riding academics'. Other European countries have been more responsive to new ideas. In 1975 the Dutch government recognised that it needed a 'steering' rather than an 'adaptive' policy

115 The *Rollfiets*, a cycle-wheelchair developed with government funding by Peter Messerschmidt, a West German lecturer in technology. The cycle section can be uncoupled and locked up, leaving the wheelchair to be pushed on foot in the standard way. The *Rollfiets* is an example of the new inventiveness and enterprise evident in West German cycle design.

towards traffic, and started a substantial programme for the building and improvement of cycle paths both in towns and across country. It is looking favourably at the recent Woonerf concept: housing communities in which motor traffic is either physically prohibited or else forced by careful road design to slow down to cycling speed, and in which all services and facilities are sited within walking or cycling distance. Dutch cycle campaigning has long been integrated with other transport issues. Discussion of new ways of living is encouraged by *Vogelvrije Fietser* (Rogue Cyclist), the radical magazine of the Echte Nederlandse Fietserbond (Genuine Dutch Federation of Cyclists).

In West Germany the bicycle has become a major component and symbol of 'alternative' politics and counter-cultural lifestyles. The more radical tend to reject excessive regimentation and consumerism in cycling matters. They mock the new 'instant clubmen' who buy identically expensive racing cycles and clothing, and tour in large groups accompanied by a baggage vehicle. The German Ministry of the Interior is co-ordinating a relatively vigorous

116 Lui Tratter (left), a radical Austrian autophobe teaching in a Frankfurt school, converted his technical studies workshop into a cycle manufactory and encouraged his pupils to build imaginative cycles. The resulting rickshaws, quadricycles, delivery tricycles, recumbents, unicycles and twin-level tandem high-wheelers attracted wide attention. Tratter has become known as the Bicycle Philosopher of Frankfurt.

117 Members of *le Monde à Bicyclette*, the Montreal-based cycle campaign, showed how much urban road-space a car requires by touring the city-centre with their bicycles surrounded by car-size wooden frames. The campaign's flair for imaginative and effective publicity has made it a model for other cycle campaign groups.

programme of cycle path construction and, by way of experiment, has designated Rosenheim and Detmold as 'cycle-friendly towns': both have been provided with a range of cycling facilities. As in Britain, official road safety campaigns are vacuous and ineffective. One, entitled 'Hello, Partner!', encouraged road users to be nice to one another.

Perhaps the world's most effective and flamboyant cycle campaign is *Le Monde à Bicyclette*, based in Montreal. One of its leading activists, Bob Silverman, espouses 'vélorution' and argues that 'when the system accepts cyclists, cyclists will accept the system'. The campaign has shown a flair for visual publicity. To highlight the fact that cyclists could not cross any of the five city bridges over the St Lawrence, the activists invited 'Moses' to stand at the riverside expounding the ten curses of the motor car and the ten virtues of the bicycle, before ordering the waters to divide and let his people cross by bicycle. The waters did not comply, but cyclists were given bridge access in 1984. Montreal cycle campaigners have also painted unofficial cycle lanes on roads and taken a range of bulky but permissible items, including a giant stuffed hippopotamus, onto the underground to show the inconsistency of banning bicycles on underground trains.

The Bicycle Network in Philadelphia acts as a nationwide information exchange for local cycling campaigns. In addition, the League of American Wheelmen, which had ceased operating in 1942, was resurrected in 1965. It has taken up the American tradition of the 'Washington Lobby', maintaining a presence in the Capital to advise and influence the national legislature. The organisation also has a network of representatives throughout the State and Congressional constituencies. To improve its image the League has been renamed 'Bicycle USA'.

Modern Cycle Sport

The major West European countries which offer least evidence of utilitarian or radical attitudes to cycling—France, Belgium and Italy—are the spiritual homelands of cycle sport. Transport politics are not the concern of cycle sport spectators, nor of the 600 or so professional cyclists whose world is rigidly conditioned by commercial considerations and the self-contained ethics of their occupation. They are typically pragmatists, of peasant or urban working-class stock. Whether an adored star or a lesser known *domestique* they contract their skills either to individual event promoters or to team sponsors seeking publicity for their vacuum-cleaners, kitchenware, cigarettes or ice-cream. Cycle sport began drawing heavily on such *extra-sportif* sponsorship during the 1950s, when sponsorship from cycle manufacturers was weakened by the depression in their industry.

The professional racing season is demanding. It is held together by a series of city-to-city races, about sixteen of which categorise themselves as 'classics'. There are also nation-tours such as, in ascending order of importance, the Tour de Suisse, the Vuelta a España, the Giro d'Italia and the Tour de France. After the Tour de France, in July, riders are released from their trade team affiliations to make an independent living from invitation rides at local track meetings and at 'criterium' races around tight town-centre road circuits. They are also free to represent their countries at the World Championships each autumn, but revert to their trade teams for a final series of autumn 'classics'. Over the winter some riders simply rest, and others make a hectic freelance living on the six-day event circuits. In February they rejoin their teams at training camps along the French or Italian Riviera.

The central event of the professional calendar, at least for the stronger trade teams, is the Tour de France, affectionately known as *la Grande Boucle*—the big loop. It is carefully composed to incorporate a variety of terrains and events, so as to exercise the specialism of sprinters, hill-climbers and time triallists. The switch from trade teams to national teams in 1930, as a result of commercial sponsors' excesses, had been impractical in operation.

118 Tom Simpson of Britain winning the World Professional Road Race Title in 1965. The British general public was largely uninterested. Simpson died on the slopes of Mont Ventoux during the 1967 Tour de France. The illegal stimulants he had (uncharacteristically) taken had rendered him vulnerable to the extreme heat and exhaustion.

It had run counter to the almost feudal loyalties which riders show to their multinational trade teams, and had been understandably unpopular with commercial sponsors. The *extra-sportif* sponsors in particular needed something of substance on which to focus their product publicity. In 1962 the Tour reverted to trade team participation and this has remained, with the exception of 1967 and 1968. The cultivation of lavishly financed and equipped trade teams, so lucrative to the Tour organisers, has made riders less self-reliant. When, in 1913, the Tour leader, Eugène Christophe, broke his front forks, he put his bicycle on his shoulder and ran seven miles back to the nearest village. Here he found a blacksmith's shop and personally welded the fork together again. He concluded the race but was penalised by the Tour organisers for accepting outside help, in that he had allowed a small boy to operate the blacksmith's bellows. Half a century later, with riders closely followed by vans carrying team mechanics and replacement hardware, Eddy Merckx punctured on the Tour and fumed impatiently while a fumbling mechanic, developing stage fright, took a full minute to change a rear wheel.

The Tour's grand and gaudy passage around France has been variously compared with that of a sovereign state, a royal progress, an itinerant army and a travelling circus. In his excellent book, *The Great Bike Race*, Geoffrey Nicholson relates how, in the 1970s, a Tour consisted of around 2000 travellers, only 120 to 140 of whom were the cyclists themselves, the rest being camp followers: officials, technicians, reporters and publicity-makers, who live off the country and, at the smaller stage towns, fill all hotel beds for thirty miles around. The Tour occupies 26,000 gendarmes and local policemen, the former providing a column of motor-cycle outriders as a guard of honour, who simply empty their holsters each time they have to accompany the Tour beyond French territory. The Tour has its own judiciary of commissaires and is accompanied by its own medical services, one unit of which administers the daily drug tests. Distinct but ever-present is the publicity caravan of vehicles mounted with giant effigies of manufacturers' products: in bathetic contrast to the epic, man-against-the-elements tone used by the media to sell the race itself. A boil on the bottom, such as that endured by Eddy Merckx in the service of an ice-cream manufacturer, becomes, in the language of the media, a rider's 'calvary'. The media coverage is overwhelming, particularly that of *L'Équipe*, a publication which continues to provide the Tour's race director, and that of *Le Parisien Libéré*, which provides its commercial director. Television and radio follow the riders intimately, and roadside spectators are happy to catch no more than a brief sight of their favourites. According to Geoffrey Nicholson,

> It's reckoned that around fifteen million people, one third of the population of France, come to the roadside each year to see the Tour pass. An unverifiable but perfectly credible figure, for especially on Sundays and Bastille Day the crowds form an almost unbroken corridor for hundreds of miles. They arrive in time to push their Renaults into a gateway, set out lunch on the edge of the field and collect their paper hats and cracker gifts from the publicity caravan, then they stay to watch the Tour which passes like a mirage in a flash of chrome and colour ... (The onlookers) turn up in the spirit less of football spectators, expecting to have the whole action laid out before them, than of rubbernecks at a state procession content to catch a glimpse of historic figures.

In the sense that the Tour is a massive superstructure built on the physical efforts of its cyclists, any use of drugs on their part lays the integrity of the whole edifice open to question. The Tour's random drug tests detect very little evidence of drug-taking. The risk of being chosen is low and, according to one rider's testimony, there is widespread use of undetectable drugs, including painkillers taken with strychnine to relieve their depressant effect. There are also allegations of hormone treatment with cortisone, and of the misapplication of cardiac and cardio-respiratory aids. Doctors, organisers and team officials have been implicated.[18] Detectable drugs caused the death of the British rider Tommy Simpson on the slopes of Mont Ventoux in the 1967 Tour. Stimulants allowed his heart to overwork until it failed.

Track racing has maintained a strong following, and is dominated by annual amateur and professional world championships. The standard elements of the sport are sprint events, individual pursuits (rider against rider, both setting off from opposite sides of the track), team pursuits, devil-take-the-hindmost races, time trialling and motor-paced races. Although track riding has always had a degree of specialisation, fair competition has been subverted by nationalist motivated development programmes in cycle technology. Many events, and especially Olympic ones, have become the preserve of those countries prepared and able to use the latest technology. While keeping within the strictures of the Union Cycliste Internationale, recent track machines have featured extensive aerodynamic styling, the result of wind-tunnel testing. Expensive and exotic metals give weight reductions, and unusual frame dimensions result from computer-designing. The riders of these exotic machines wear one-piece skinsuits and tapered-back helmets. A German critic of the expensive NASA-aided US cycle development programme for the 1984 Los Angeles Olympics wondered whether the next scientific improvement might be some form of gene-mutation to produce riders with more aerodynamic bodies.[19] The increasing role played by sports technology, at the expense of raw human achievement, is well exemplified by the speed record attempts of Francesco Moser. When he broke a cycling world speed record in 1984 it was with the help of unreserved technical and logistical support from his commercial sponsors, and with the help of the thinner air found in Mexico.

Six-day racing, which had died out in America in the 1930s, continued in the velodromes of Europe but reached a low ebb in the 1950s and 60s. Improved conditions for the riders had weakened the event's garish attraction as a public ordeal, without any effective attempt to offer a more varied or exciting programme in compensation. Attendances fell and, during events, the velodromes became the resort of homeless drunks and black-tied socialites extending their post-party revelries. In the late 1960s and 1970s the six-day was successfully revived, with attractive, diverse race programmes, each held together by daily instalments of a Madison event, in which two-man teams score points for various feats. The London Six-Day was re-started in 1967, but lapsed in 1981, and the Paris Six-Day, formerly the high-spot of the six-day calendar, was re-started in 1984 after a twenty-five year gap, following the demolition of the old Vélodrome d'Hiver. The riders in six-day events usually work on a freelance basis. They lead a

119 A US Olympic track rider on a machine with computer-designed dimensions, a disc rear wheel, a judiciously drilled-out seat-pillar and a stay-wire. Bicycles such as these tend to represent competition between technologies rather than between riders.

120 Prepared for serious business, the Americans Lon Haldeman and his wife, Susan Noterangelo, wait for the start of an annual Ride Across America event. The route stretches from the Pacific to the Atlantic: 3000 miles of mountains, deserts and plains. It can be covered in nine days by leading riders: around 330 miles per day.

nomadic existence travelling from track to track during the hectic four-month winter season. Their income must cover the expenses of running a car and of employing, feeding and accommodating a two- or three-man back-up team.[20]

In Japan a genre of track racing known as Keirin, initiated in 1948, attracts

40 million spectators a year to fifty velodromes. The competitors start, like greyhounds, from stalls, and chase after a single pacer on a motor-cycle who comes from behind them. The 'hare' gradually winds up the pace and, with about a lap and a half to go, leaves the track, this being the signal for the final and often dangerous sprint to start. The prize money is high and the betting, at four billion pounds per year, provides a high income for local municipal governments and for the Association of Keirin, founded in 1957 to train riders and regulate the sport. It has 4000 registered riders, each a graduate of the Association's expensively equipped training school. The income from betting levies has also provided abundant funding for a resplendent 'bicycle-centre', including a museum of cycling, in Tokyo.[21]

In the USA the revival of competitive cycling has taken some imaginative forms, many of which allow amateur recreational cyclists to take part. They include ultra-marathon, triathlon, mountain bike, HPV and BMX events. Other developments include the RAAM (Ride Across America), the Tour of America, and a resurgence of track racing. American cycle sport supports a growing number of professional riders, some of whom take part in prestigious European road events, where traditional continental dominance has been upset by successful English-speaking professionals from Australia, Ireland and Britain, as well as from America: all countries without strong traditions of organised road racing.

British road racing, long stifled by British cycling's governing bodies, had been kept alive in the 1930s by events on private roads such as the motor racing tracks at Brooklands and Donnington. But it was in 1942 that Percy Stallard ended the exile of British riders from open-road competitions as practised on the Continent. He organised a mass-start cycle race from Llangollen to Wolverhampton in defiance of the National Cyclists' Union and the Road Time-Trials Council, but with the co-operation of the police forces en route. Stallard was immediately banned from the NCU for life but later in the same year formed the British League of Racing Cyclists. Many of the wartime clubmen were teenagers. They tended to be more racing-minded than their conscripted elders, and welcomed Stallard's initiative. Some NCU clubs defected en masse, and others divided into two sections, one riding under NCU rules and the other engaged in mass-start road racing under the British League of Racing Cyclists. The police co-operated, road behaviour was good, and road racing thrived. The British League of Racing Cyclists represented both amateurs and professionals and was responsible for organising the Tour of Britain, an amateur event which first took place in 1952 and which later became known as the Milk Race. After much ill-will the BLRC and the NCU were amalgamated in 1959, becoming the British Cycling Federation which controls cycle sport to this day.[22] Despite Percy Stallard's efforts, cycle sport was not able to greatly broaden its public following until the arrival of Channel Four Television which began broadcasting city centre 'criterium' events in 1983, sponsored by Kelloggs.

Perhaps stimulated by developments in road racing, time trialling recovered well from the war and remains a sport in which newcomers of all abilities can compete against their personal best. Black alpacas and tights are no longer *de rigeur*. The official records of the Road Time-Trials Council, as well as those of the Road Records Association, testify to the achievements of road engineers as well as of competitors. Heavy traffic can also help, thanks to the suction effect of passing lorries. Ten of the top twelve time triallists in the 1976 Best British All-Rounder competition for amateurs clocked up their best times for the fifty and hundred mile events on one particularly busy and well-surfaced section of the A1 in Yorkshire.[23] Beryl Burton, an amateur often described as the most successful woman athlete ever, began her varied cycling career as a time triallist and still trains daily on the A1 in Yorkshire. From 1959 for two decades she excelled in all aspects of women's cycling at international level.

Amateur cycle sport benefits the many who are active, and professional cycling gives pleasure to those who follow their heroes from grandstands or in the pages of *Cycling* and *Winning*. Although both remain minority activities it may be that the strength and variety of the revived American interest in cycle sport will give a boost to cycle sport in Britain. This has already been the case with human-powered vehicle racing, BMX, mountain-bike events and triathlons.

Cycling in the Third World

During the 1970s the social and ecological advantages of cycling were given a radical intellectual rationale by Ivan Illich. He argued that Third World countries face a choice. They can opt for an equitable, undistorting, 'intermediate' technology involving, amongst other things, bicycle transportation on inexpensive networks of tracks between farms, villages and local market places; or they can import prestigious large-scale western transport technology which needs a constant supply of fuel, spares and service-skills from abroad, and which benefits lorry and car owners at the direct expense of the already underprivileged. Even such a straightforward matter as the improvement of rural roads in Bangladesh and Nepal gave such a great competitive advantage to the larger, motorised, farmers and traders, that they impoverished many unmotorised peasants and were able to buy up the latters' land.[24]

The principal Third World transport activity is the carrying of vital goods, such as farm produce, water and firewood: by means of one's head, hands and shoulders, or by bullock-cart. A World Bank study in Kenya showed that most transport needs were for the movement of small loads (20

121 A participant in the welcoming ceremony for Queen Elizabeth in Tonga, December 1953, cycles back to his village with his wife alongside. With the notable exception of China, cycling in the Third World is principally a male occupation.

to 300 pounds weight) over short distances (eleven to fifteen miles): conditions easily met by cycle transport.[25] In Illich's view, any society which cannot provide each of its citizens with a bicycle should be regarded as under-equipped, yet few Third World governments have encouraged local bicycle production, while forty-seven of them had established automobile industries by 1972. Inappropriate technology has been imported for reasons which are misguided as often as they are base. The middle classes of some Third World countries have come to suspect, without apparent reason, that the developed world, through the World Bank, promotes intermediate technology in order to prevent the underdeveloped world from establishing a heavy industrial base which might prove too competitive.

The design of the Third World roadster bicycle has changed little since the days when an enthusiasm for wheeling passed from colonial officials to native potentates, long before it became a tool for survival to tens of millions. An early example of the commercial carriage of goods by bicycle occurred in Eastern Nigeria in the 1930s. In the previous decade palm oil had been transported by light lorries to the European trading depots at railheads and the coast. But when the price of the product fell, cyclists took over, strapping up to three four-gallon tins of oil onto their British-built bicycles. In 1934 one district officer reported that 'the entire transport of palm oil and much of the passenger traffic is in the hands of native cyclists with the results that lorries are being laid off the roads.'[26] By 1942 over 60,000 men were employed taking palm oil to export points, and returning with goods such as kerosene and stockfish. The East Nigerians had become bicycle-minded. They formed co-operative clubs to buy bicycles and they established private-enterprise bicycle transportation stations throughout the area, where passengers and goods could be picked up (presumably on tricycles). By the 1950s the railways and lorries had re-appropriated much of the palm oil and passenger traffic, but the bicycle continues to play a significant role in both trades.[27]

In Bogota, Columbia, a major bakery had constant problems maintaining the ninety vans which it used for supplying its 20,000 sales outlets. In about 1983 it replaced its van fleet with 1200 carrier tricycles and found that distribution costs fell from 27 per cent to 8 per cent of total costs. There was also a large increase in sales, mainly because the tricycles could, unlike vans, manoeuvre effectively through stagnant traffic, making deliveries more reliable. The bakery's initiative also created over a thousand new jobs.[28] Cycles are used extensively for delivery work in other Latin American cities. The riders of Mexico City, where the average traffic flow in the

122 A family, possibly going to market; on a standard roadster by BSA.

city-centre is two miles per hour, have earned a reputation for the size of loads which they balance on their racks, handlebars and heads.

In some Third World countries high levels of cycling in cities is perceived as a problem by the authorities. After years of restriction by the Indonesian government Jakarta's 40,000 remaining *becaks*—tricycle rickshaw taxis on which the driver sits behind the passengers—have been banned on the grounds that they represent a hazard and obstruction to other traffic. The state governor suggested that the redundant *becak* drivers might be trained to drive cars. 'That', an Indonesian journalist remarked, 'would certainly give them a skill not possessed by taxi-drivers'.[29] In Penang, Malaysia, there are 1700 registered tricycle rickshaw (trishaw) pedallers. They offer tourist services, monthly contracts for taking children to school, fixed rates for carrying foodstuffs or laundry, and a fixed rate for proceeding slowly with passengers from the maternity wing of the hospital. Impulse journeys are catered for by cruising trishaw-pedallers. Trishaws offer a cheap, personal, responsive, pollution-free form of transport, and have no need of expensively imported petrol. Yet they are being suppressed, ostensibly because of their alleged association with petty theft and drug-trafficking, and because they obstruct faster traffic. The more likely reason for wanting to sweep this poor man's technology out of sight is that the trishaws of Penang, in common with the *becaks* of Jakarta, present to overseas visitors an image of underdevelopment in countries which are outgrowing third world status.[30] The strange attitude to bicycles in Abu Dhabi (United Arab Emirates) may also fit into this pattern. In about October 1981 the Interior Minister banned cycling on the main streets of the Capital, at any time of day, on the grounds that cyclists were causing too many accidents. Those who ignored the ban had their cycles confiscated, and, a year later, the central police station looked out over a graveyard of 3000 rusting bicycles.[31]

However useful the trishaw may be, it has also led to exploitation which has brought daily misery to many of those it employs. In India trishaw drivers work up to twelve hours per day and are expected to carry up to two men and their loads in temperatures as high as a hundred degrees Fahrenheit. Yet low incomes leave the drivers (and their families) malnourished. Being thus more prone to diseases, drivers are lucky to reach the age of forty. The majority of Indian trishaw drivers hire their vehicles from professional trishaw owners, who can recoup their capital expenditure on one machine within six months, whereas it will be on the road for around ten years.

A much quoted dictum amongst Third World socialists is that of a minister in the short-lived socialist government of Salvador Allende in Chile: 'Socialism can only be achieved on a bicycle'.[32] Socialist governments of Africa and South America have emphasised the role of the bicycle as an instrument of social change. In Tanzania the government of Julius Nyerere

123 A Delhi rickshaw carrying rolls of paper.

124 Carrying children to school in Delhi. Some 'school-bus' trishaws have an enclosed passenger section with windows.

began importing large numbers of bicycles around 1955. But in 1978 a bicycle factory was built in the capital, Dar es Salaam, which began producing the 'Swala', or 'National Bicycle'. By 1980 the factory was self-sufficient: only the steel was imported. Bicycles are essential to Tanzania's decentralised health programme. Health workers cycle to communities within a seven mile radius of rural health centres. Although such track-cycling is arduous, bicycles enable vaccines to be transported a greater distance before the heat destroys them. Oxfam and UNICEF have bought 'Swala' bicycles for Tanzanian health workers, and Oxfam has published a repair manual especially for them. Much of the decentralised medical care in this desperately poor country is preventative, but patients needing specialised care can be transported to hospital on cycle-trailers. Such bush ambulances are also used in Nigeria, the Cameroons and elsewhere. Unfortunately, a few years after Tanzania's National Cycle Company had been established, it became clear that the country did not have the resources to sustain manufacture and the factory was closed down. Cycles were again imported, 120,000 of them in 1984 alone.

Bicycle manufacture or assembly plants have been set up in more recently established and more embattled socialist states, such as Nicaragua, Mozambique and Angola. Nicaragua has also been receiving bicycles for its teachers, health workers and union officials from 'Bikes not Bombs' campaigns in the United States and Britain.

In China there are around 180 million bicycles: seventy of them to every motorised vehicle. A bicycle is a very serious investment, costing the equivalent of three to four months' average pay. Some purchasers are so protective that their new machines are ridden with pieces of cardboard wrapping still in place. Cycle-commuters receive a monthly travel allowance equivalent to a day's income for a manual worker. In a typical city about 50 per cent of cyclists receive this subsidy, which in the course of four years can pay off the initial cost of the bicycle, leaving the cyclist with a net income from then on. All cycles must be registered and display licences, which minimises cycle-theft. In addition, cycles are left, individually locked up, in supervised cycle parking enclosures. There is a debate as to whether the subsidy might not be better spent on improving public transport, since buses (which are almost always crowded) take up a road area of one to two square metres per person carried, as opposed to the six to ten square metres needed for a cyclist. So torrential are the rivers of cyclists in cities—50,000 per hour (fourteen per second) on some roads—that even the use of twenty-foot-wide cycle lanes either side of a motor traffic lane can no longer prevent buses, and also lorries, from being slowed down to cycling pace. Buses are about the only form of transport available to the seventy per cent of city dwellers who do not have regular access to a bicycle, and slowness, combined with overcrowding, make urban buses less able to attract riders from their bicycles. So troublesome is this vicious circle in traffic management that at least one local authority, Peking, is actively discouraging cycling in urban areas and is moving workers to jobs closer to their homes.

125 The ubiquitous Chinese bicycle: not a car in sight.

Cycling in China does not appear to be particularly safe. Fifty per cent of all reported accidents to the person involve bicycles, and a recent western visitor reported seeing five cyclists killed in accidents during one three-day trip.[33] Cyclists have traditionally ignored motor users, even lorry drivers blasting air-horns to clear the way. But cycling is coming under increasing regulation, and no longer does the prime responsibility for avoiding accidents rest with the motor user. The continuing national commitment to cycling is practical and appropriate. Private motoring, however, is no longer the crime that it once was. Public officials enjoy their motor cars of office, and when Sun Guiying, a woman chicken farmer, managed to sell a record number of eggs, she was not only officially honoured, but also allowed to use her earnings to become Peking's first peasant to own a motor car.

China produces about 32,000,000 cycles per year, and production is rising at a rate of about forty-five per cent a year. Most of the products of this expansion are exported, although the level of cycling in China itself is rising at about twelve per cent per year. Principal brand names are 'Flying Dove', 'Five Rams', 'White Mountain', 'Red Flag' and 'Eternity'. These are standard roadsters, equipped with bells but rarely with gears, crated to local cycle workshops for assembly. Very recently lighter bicycles, made entirely in factories, have appeared in the cities. They have various wheel-sizes and are painted in colours other than utility black. There is still a great deal of specialised cycle manufacture: tricycles are built to carry goods such as timber, cotton, furniture, sewing machines, firewood, livestock, and even to carry tankfuls of sewage from the cities for use on outlying farms. Children travel in bicycle side-cars, but tricycle-rickshaw travel is not common.[34]

The creative use of load-carrying cycles is an example of how the Chinese have, through necessity and independent-mindedness, developed the possibilities of cycle transport to a full extent. The standard Chinese roadster is bringing cheap, private but social transport to a rapidly increasing proportion of society: an example which has heartened the 'new cyclists' in the West. China is industrialising, but with cycle manufacture much to the fore, and it is with a commitment to cycling that the nation approaches world influence. The outcome for cycling cannot be predicted, but may well be exciting.

POSTSCRIPT

THE DIVERSE HISTORY of cycling shows it to be, like walking, an irrepressible and adaptive activity. This is not surprising since the human on a bicycle is, in terms of energy expended in relation to the rider's body-weight and distance travelled, the most efficient of all moving animals and machines. The bicycle is designed around the human figure, so that the most powerful muscles are used in the most effective way. Unlike motor cars, bicycles are accessible to nearly everyone, and benefit riders without harming others. Motor vehicles off-load their enormous social costs onto the community as a whole: they mean restricted mobility for the carless, the destruction of neighbourhoods, damaged and devalued property, road-building costs, lost agricultural land, police and court resources tied up, social services, hospital care for the injured, noxious exhaust fumes, airborne lead, asbestos dust from car brakes, acid rain, noise pollution, and a national dependence on imported Middle Eastern oil. Apart from all this there is the unforgivable social cost of the 250,000 deaths on British roads since 1945. Drivers become victims of their own machines, or, in Illich's words, 'captive consumers of conveyance'. Some become dangerously desensitised: brutalised by the excessive speed and power put at their disposal. Yet we have become a car-culture, and shape accordingly our physical environment and way of life. This process has been encouraged by successive governments. For example, the tax subsidy given to company cars is greater than the entire public transport subsidy.

The bicycle is the vehicle of a new mentality. It quietly challenges a system of values which condones dependency, wastage, inequality of mobility and daily carnage. Cycling provides little scope for self-aggrandisement, consumerism or big-business profit: it is perhaps too simple, cheap and independent for its own good in this age of excess. The recent cycling boom has been a heartening resurgence of the human spirit. It needs, however, to be encouraged by government intervention. Motorists' behaviour needs to be more effectively controlled so that their much vaunted 'freedom to choose' no longer eclipses the freedoms of pedestrians, cyclists and others. Also, heavy goods vehicles, which demolish any claim we have to civilisation, need to be severely restricted. A fraction of the public resources spent on coping with motor traffic could finance networks of safe, uninterrupted cycleways in towns and across country, complemented by enhanced railway and urban public transport systems. Many millions more would then be able to make cycling an important and pleasurable part of their daily lives, at the same time improving the quality of life for all of us. Such facilities might well pay for themselves in terms of savings made by a lower level of motoring. Cycling is a boon to society and to ignore it is expensive. There is every reason why cycling should be helped to enjoy another Golden Age.

SOURCE NOTES

CHAPTER ONE

1 *Leonardo da Vinci: L'Automobile e la Bicicletta*, Augusto Marinoni. A less detailed English language account is given by Marinoni in a chapter of *Leonardo the Scientist*, Carlo Zammattio. See also 'Leonardo and the Bicycle', J. McGurn, *Bicycle Magazine*, June 1983, pp. 38–41; and in 'The Leonardo Debate', (similarly), September 1983, pp. 25–29.

2 *Mit dem Rad durch zwei Jahrhunderte*, Rauck, Volke, Paturi, pp. 10, 11; *Velocipeden, Automobilen och Motorcykeln*, Hubendick, pp. 458–461.

3 *La Vie Parisienne*, Almera, pp. 109–111.

4 A 'genealogy' of hobby-horse design is provided in 'Laufrad—Vélocipède—Hobby-horse. Eine typologische Untersuchung', Plath.

5 *Vélocipèdes*, Lockert, 1896, pp. 54, 55.

6 Quoted by Dunham, 'The Bicycle Era in American History', p. 11. Source date unknown.

7 Quoted without source in 'Velocipedes: their Fluctuations in Public Favour', an undated article of the 1880s, reprinted in the *Boneshaker*, 109, Spring 1985, pp. 11–21.

8 Quoted thus by various US periodicals of the time. Original London source unknown. (Dunham, p. 20.)

9 Dunham, p. 19.

10 Quoted by Dunham, p. 14, source unknown.

11 Above details of monocycles and other US inventions from Dunham, XI–XIX.

12 *Fahrradpatente*, Herzog, p. 55 and p. 65.

13 Lefèbvre's bicycle was rediscovered and researched by Andrew Ritchie. His account is in the *Boneshaker*, no. 81, vol. 9, Winter 1975, pp. 5–18.

CHAPTER TWO

1 'The Latest Parisian Whim', *London Society*, vol 14, 1868, pp. 408–414.

2 From a later English manual, *The Veloce*, anon., Reynolds and Mays, 1869.

3 The catalogue of the 1867 World Fair makes no reference to velocipede exhibits. Michaux very probably exhibited his wares in the grounds. (See note 15.)

4 *Vélocipède Illustré*, 1 April 1869. The magazine is held on microfilm at Boston Spa National Lending Library.

5 Ibid.

6 Ibid., 22 April 1869.

7 Ibid., 8 April 1869.

8 Quoted in *Een Eeuw Wijzer*, ANWB, p. 10.

9 Lallement may have worked for Michaux at some time, although he himself denied it. In 1894 Michaux's son, Henri, claimed that Lallement had, in 1865, been 'employed to improve the imperfections of the machine' (his own words, taken from an interview with an American visitor, published in *Leslie's Weekly*, 27 June 1895, quoted by Dunham, p. IX).

10 *Ten Thousand Miles on a Bicycle*, Karl Kron, p. 400.

11 *Velocipedes*, anon, USA, 1869, p. 24.

12 *Detroit Post*, 16 June 1869; Dunham, p. 139.

13 *Detroit Post*, 6 May 1869; Dunham, p. 139.

14 The information in this paragraph is from 'Growth and Entrepreneurship in the British Cycle Industry', A. Harrison.

15 Information in this paragraph is from the *Nottinghamshire Guardian*, 9 February 1918.

16 Mayall's companions finished the journey by coach, which they took to at Crawley. It was at Crawley that *The Times* man turned back. Did they wait until *The Times* man had gone? His report fails to mention the change of transport.

CHAPTER THREE

1 *The Cyclist*, 24 May 1882, pp. 397, 398.

2 *The Wheelman* (US) May 1883, p. 162.

3 *History of the Pickwick Bicycle Club*, Crushton, p. 2.

4 From the Hon. Keith-Falconer's diary of a Land's End to John o'Groat's tour, June 1882, quoted by Sinker, p. 128.

5 Quoted in *The Cyclist*, 4 October 1882.

6 *The Cyclist*, 30 November 1881.

7 *Fifty Years of Road Riding*, Moxham, p. 12.

8 *Turnpike Road to Tartan Track* (The Story of Northern Foot Handicaps), Moffatt, passim.

9 Quoted by Bailey, *Leisure and Class in Victorian England*. Much of my information is drawn from chap. 6: 'Rational Recreation and the New Athleticism'.

10 Correspondence from Keith-Falconer to his mother and sister, July 1881, quoted by Sinker, p. 117.

11 *Cycle-Clips*, Sinclair, pp. 14–23.

12 *Mémoires de Terront*, Terront and de Saunier, pp. 61, 62.

13 *Bicyclist's Handbook*, 1879, pp. 90–93.

14 *Cycling Mercury*, 1 October 1883.

15 Quoted by S. S. McClure, *My Autobiography*, p. 145.

16 Smith, pp. 9–11; McClure, pp. 145–152; Adams, pp. 55–122, passim.

17 *De Kampioen*, June 1885.

18 From a letter from Monsieur Albin, published in *The Cyclist*, 28 June 1882. He was a circus high bicycle gymnast, then on a solo publicity tour of the United States.

19 Details from Dunham, p. 261.

CHAPTER FOUR

1 *The Velocipede*, Bottomley-Firth, pp. 50, 51.

2 Quoted by Derek Roberts, *The Boneshaker*, 66, Spring 1972.

3 *The Cyclist*, 12 April 1882, p. 315.
4 *The Wheel (Supplement)*, USA, 9 May 1884, quoted by Dunham.
5 *The Cyclist*, 28 June 1882.
6 *Cosmopolitan* 29 August 1895, quoted by Dunham.
7 Dunham, pp. 221, 222.
8 *Sewing Machine Gazette*, 1 November 1881, p. 24.
9 *Mit dem Rad durch zwei Jahrhunderte*, Rauck, pp. 147, 148.
10 *Cycling Mercury*, 1 September 1883.

CHAPTER FIVE

1 The race is described in *Mémoires de Terront*, Terront and de Saunier.
2 *Cyclette Revue: histoire chronologique du cyclisme*, February, 1961. Quoted by Holt.
3 *On Forsythe's Change*, Heinemann, 1930, p. 207.
4 *Potternewton Cycling Club Monthly Record*, October 1891. Issues April 1891 to October 1895 are kept at Leeds City Library.
5 *The Cyclist*, 5 September 1888.
6 Run, bicycle, run, in the radiance which is yours/It is progress which is sitting on your saddle. From *Ode au Vélocipède*, quoted by Weber in 'Gymnastics and Sports' (see [7]).
7 A full account of the subject is in 'Gymnastics and Sports in Fin-de-Siècle France: Opium of the Classes?', Eugen Weber, *American History Review*, vol 76, part 1, 1971, pp. 70–98.
8 Ibid., pp. 122, 123.
9 *Fahrrad und Radfahrer*, Wilhelm Wolf, p. 238 (of 1980 reprint).
10 *Das Radfahren und seine Hygiene*, Dr med. Schiefferdecker.
11 *An Autobiography*, Theodore Roosevelt, Scribner, New York, 1925. Quoted by Harmond.
12 Adams, pp. 164–206, passim.
13 'The Bicycle Boom of the 1890s', Gary A. Tobin, *Journal of Popular Culture*, 7, Spring 74, pp. 838–849.
14 *Bicycling News*, 23 September 1893.
15 *The Bicycle and the Bush* is the source of almost all my information on the history of cycling in Australia. I am indebted to Jim Fitzpatrick.
16 Quoted without source, *de Fiets*, Fuchs and Simon, p. 41.
17 *Handbuch des Radfahr-Sport*, Moritz Band, Vienna, 1895.
18 *Vanity Fair*, 11 June 1896.
19 *Century Magazine* (US), August 1897.
20 *I Have Been Young*, Helena Swanwick, Gollancz, 1935. Quoted by Rubenstein.
21 *Radical Dress Society Gazette*, July 1888.
22 *The Clarion*, 7 September 1895. The writer lived in Manchester. Quoted by Rubenstein.
23 *From Ritual to Record*, Guttmann, p. 61.
24 *Sport and Society in Modern France*, Holt. The information in this paragraph is from chapter five: 'Cycling as a Commercial Spectacle'.
25 According to F. Perriman, writing in the *Windsor Magazine*, vol. 6, p. 537, the coat trick happened 'very frequently'.

26 *Social History of Cycling*, Smith, p. 159.
27 *Le Cyclisme*, Laget, p. 40.
28 From *Society Ladies Awheel*, Derek Roberts. One of five sets of slides on the history of cycling, the Slide Centre, Ilminster, Somerset.

CHAPTER SIX

1 *My Life and Times*, Jerome K. Jerome, p. 68.
2 *The Hub*, 9 Jan. 1897, p. 400.
3 *Badminton Magazine*, April 1897, pp. 393–400.
4 *The Hub*, 6 February 1897, pp. 25, 26.
5 *Love among the Butterflies*, Margaret Fountaine.
6 *The Banquet Years*, Roger Shattuck, p. 10.
7 *One Hundred Years of Bicycle Posters*, Jack Rennert, pp. 3, 4.
8 The Race forms a chapter in Jarry's surrealist novel, *The Supermale*.
9 *The Hub*, 12 March 1898; *Illustrirte Zeitung*, 31 October 1896.
10 *De Fiets*, Fuchs and Simon, p. 48. My translation.
11 'Progress and Flight', Harmond, *Journal of Social History*, p. 241.
12 All details in this paragraph from *Social History of Cycling*, Smith, p. 48.
13 'Social and Economic Influence of the Bicycle', *Forum* (US periodical), August 1898, pp. 680–689.
14 *The Americans: a Social History*, Furness, p. 811.
15 'Competitiveness of the British Cycle Industry', Harrison, *Econ. Hist. Review*.
16 *Veertig Jaar*, anonymous, 1923. A jubilee publication for the Algemeen Nederlandsche Wielrijders-Bond.
17 'Gymnastics and Sport', Weber, p. 81; *Sport and Society in Modern France*, Holt, p. 185.
18 Correspondence from the Workers' Cycling Federation's press committee to the British Clarion Cycling Club (24 May 1913), Manchester Studies, archives.
19 *Das Wilhelminische Berlin*, Annemarie Lange, pp. 547–554.
20 *The Scout*, May 1895, p. 16, quoted by Rubenstein, 'Cycling in the 1890s', to which I am indebted for various information.
21 *England 1870 to 1914*, R. K. C. Ensor, Oxford, 1941, p. 334.
22 *The Scout*, January 1896, quoted in Judith Fincher's interesting dissertation on the Clarion movement (see Bibliography), to which I am indebted for various information.
23 *The Hub*, 8 August 1896, p. 6.
24 From the Introduction to *What's all This?*, Blatchford, 1940.
25 'The Clarion Clubs', David Prynn, *Journal of Contemporary History*, p. 68.
26 *Social History of Cycling*, Smith, p. 119.
27 Ibid., pp. 136, 137: for various details of six-day races.
28 *Edwardian Excursions*, edited from Benson's diaries by David Newsome, p. 1.
29 From a tape-recorded interview by the Ripon Community History Project, 1 November 83.
30 *This Great Club of Ours*, CTC, 1953.

CHAPTER SEVEN

1 *Nottingham Evening Post*, 9 February 1926.

2 Quoted by Woodforde, *Story of the Bicycle*.

3 *English Journey*, J. B. Priestley, Jubilee edn., Heinemann, 1984, p. 135.

4 *Experiment in Autobiography*, H. G. Wells; quoted by MacKenzie.

5 Transcription of a tape-recorded interview, 21 January 1984, York Oral History Project.

6 *Newcastle Evening Chronicle*, 15 May 1984.

7 Personal communications, February 1985.

8 'Hats off to the Errand Boy!', *Cycling*, 28 June 1939, from which parts of the subsequent information are taken.

9 *Die Gartenlaube*, 1902, quoted by Francke, *Lob des Fahrrads*.

10 'Paul Evett, compositor': an autobiographical contribution to *Useful Toil*, ed. by John Burnett, Allen Lane, 1974, p. 334.

11 *Summoned by Bells*, 1960; quoted by MacKenzie.

12 *The Captain*, vol. 8, 1903, p. 446.

13 *The Motor Car and Politics*, Plowden, p. 241.

14 'The Cyclist in the House', Lynn Atterbury, *Cyclist Monthly*, June 1983, p. 21.

15 In evidence to Alness Committee, Hansard, Lords, 192, July 1938, 3850–6, quoted by Plowden.

16 *L'Auto-Vélo*, 5 April 1901, quoted by Jacques Seray: 'Et Desgrange créa le Tour', in *le Cycle*, July/August 1982.

17 Holt, pp. 96–102; Durry, pp. 48–53 passim; Nicholson, pp. 48–55.

CHAPTER EIGHT

1 Quoted by William Plowden, *Motor Car and Politics*, p. 379.

2 Ibid., pp. 331, 332.

3 *The Needless Scourge*, Plowden and Hillman, p. 152.

4 'The Future of the Bicycle in a Modern Society', *Journal of the Royal Society of Arts*, January 1968, pp. 114–134: the text of a paper read by E. C. Claxton, Chief Engineer, Stevenage Development Corporation, with related debate.

5 *Traffic in Towns* (the 'Buchanan Report'), Ministry of Transport, 1963.

6 *The Moulton Bicycle*, Hadland, p. 34.

7 'The Rallying of Raleigh', C. Mansell, *Management Today*, February 1973, p. 88, quoted by Open University Course Team in *Bicycles: Invention and Innovation*.

8 Ibid. (Mansell), pp. 85, 88.

9 *Bicycle USA*, July/August 1985, from the annual survey of the Bicycle Federation.

10 *Bicycles and Public Transportation*, M. A. Replongle, 1983.

11 *Bicycle Action*, London, January/February 1986, pp. 5, 6.

12 Information in the above paragraph from *Bicycles: Invention and Innovation*, Open University, pp. 93, 94.

13 Sheila Webb, *Daily Cyclist*, London, September 1984, p. 3.

14 *Bicycle Magazine*, London, January/February 1982, p. 48.

15 Radio Four 'phone-in', 10 December 1985.

16 Address to the Bow Group, quoted by the *New Statesman*, 29 June 1984.

17 'Cycling in Towns: A Quantitative Investigation', J. R. Waldman, LRT1 Working Paper 3, December 1977.

18 *The Great Bike Race*, Nicholson, pp. 100, 101.

19 *Radfahren*, Bielefeld, September/October 1984, p. 4.

20 'Six-Day Racing', *Bicycle Action*, London, January/February 1986, pp. 34–37.

21 'Kierin', *Bicycle Action*, London, May 1985, pp. 31–37.

22 Information in the above paragraph is from *Centenary 78: the Story of 100 Years of organised British Cycle Racing*, Henderson, pp. 83–89.

23 *The Penguin Book of the Bicycle*, Watson and Grey, p. 218.

24 *New Internationalist*, October 1980, p. 9, no original source given.

25 Ibid., p. 13, no original source given.

26 Memo by H. Waddington, D.O., 16 January 1934, quoted by A. Nwabughuogu (see next note).

27 'The Role of Bicycle Transportation in the Economic Development of Eastern Nigeria', A. Nwabughuogu, *Journal of Transport History* (US), March 1884, pp. 91–97.

28 *Network News* (US), 23, July–September 1984, pp. 28, 29.

29 *New York Times*, 15 December 1984.

30 'Pedalling in Penang', Peter Rimmer, *New Internationalist*, Oct. 1980, p. 15.

31 *Khaleej Times* (United Arab Emirates), 4 August 1982.

32 'El socialismo puede llegar solo en bicicleta': José Antonio Viera-Gallo, Assistant Secretary of Justice in Allende's Government.

33 *Asiaweek*, 16 July 1982.

34 My major source of information on cycling in China has been 'Bicycle Traffic in China', Jun-Meng Yang, *Transportation Quarterly* (US), January 1985, pp. 93–107.

BIBLIOGRAPHY

Almera, Henri d', *La Vie Parisienne sous la Restauration*, Albin Michel, Paris, 1910

Alderson, Federick, *Bicycling, A History*, David and Charles, London, 1974

Algemeene Nederlandsche Wielrijdersbond, *Een Eeuw Wijzer, 100 Jaar ANWB 1883–1983*, ANWB, The Hague, 1983

Adams, G. Donald, *Collecting and Restoring Antique Bicycles*, TAB Books, Pennsylvania, USA, 1981

Bailey, Peter, *Leisure and Class in Victorian England*, Routledge and Kegan Paul, London, 1978

Band, Moritz, *Handbuch des Radfahr-Sports*, Vienna, 1895

Barthes, Roland, *Mythologies*, Editions du Seuil, Paris, 1957

Bartleet, Samuel, *Bartleet's Bicycle Book*, Burrow and Co., London, 1931; reprinted by the Pinkerton Press, Birmingham, 1983

Bellencontre, Paraclèse, *Hygiène du Vélocipède*, Paris, 1869 (Brit. Lib.)

Benson, A. C., *Edwardian Excursions* (diary extracts, ed. by David Newsome), John Murray, London, 1981

Borge, Jacques and Viasnoff, Nicolas, *Le Vélo, la Liberté*, Balland, Paris, 1978

Bottomley-Firth, J. F., *The Velocipede. Its Past, Present and its Future*, London, 1869

Caunter, C. F., *Cycles, History and Development*, H. M. Stationery Office, 1955

Crushton, the Hon., ?, *History of the Pickwick Bicycle Club*, the Pickwick Bicycle Club, 1905

Cyclists' Touring Club, *This Great Club of Ours*, CTC, 1953

Dunham, Norman, 'The Bicycle Era in American History', unpublished doctoral thesis, Harvard University, 1956

Durry, Jean, *La véridique Histoire des Géants de la Route*, Denoel, Paris, 1973

Ebeling, Hermann, *Der Freiherr von Drais*, G. Braun, Karlsruhe, 1985

Evans, David E., *The Ingenious Mr Pedersen*, Alan Sutton, Dursley, 1979

Fincher, Judith, 'The Clarion Movement: a Study of a Socialist Attempt to Implement the Co-operative Commonwealth in England, 1891–1914', unpublished M.A. dissertation, Univ. of Manchester, 1971

Fitzpatrick, Jim, *The Bicycle and the Bush*, Oxford Univ. Press, Melbourne, 1980

Fountaine, Margaret, *Love among the Butterflies* (diary extracts ed. by W. F. Cater), Collins, London, 1980

Francke, Peter, *Lob des Fahrrads*, Sanssouci, Zürich, 1974

Fraser, J. Foster, *Round the World on a Wheel*, Nelson, London, 1899. Reprinted by Chatto, 1982

Fuchs, J. and Simon, W., *de Fiets*, Museum Boymans-van Beuningen, Rotterdam, 1977

Furnas, Joseph C., *The Americans: a Social History of the United States*, Longmans, London, 1970

Grew, W., *The Cycle Industry*, London, Pitman, 1921

Guttmann, Allen, *From Ritual to Record*, Columbia Univ. Press, New York, 1978

Hadland, Tony, *The Moulton Bicycle*, 2nd edn, privately published, Reading (UK), 1982

Harmond, Richard, 'Progress and Flight: an Interpretation of the American Cycle Craze of the 1890s', *Journal of Social History*, vol. 5, 1971–72, pp. 235–257

Harrison, Anthony E., 'Growth, Entrepreneurship and Capital Formation in the U.K. Cycle and related Industries, 1870–1914', unpublished doctoral thesis, Univ. of York, 1977

Harrison, Anthony E., 'Competitiveness in the British Cycle Industry, 1890–1914', *Economic History Review*, 2nd ser., 22, August 1969, pp. 287–303.

Henderson, Noel G., *Centenary 78: The Story of 100 Years of Organised British Cycle Racing*, Kennedy Bros, Silsden (UK), 1977

Herzog, Ulrich, *Fahrradpatente*, Moby Dick Verlag, Kiel, 1984

Hillier, G. Lacy, *Cycling*, Badminton Library, Longmans, Green and Co., London, 1889 (and many other editions)

Holt, Richard, *Sport and Society in Modern France*, MacMillan, London, 1981

Hubendick, Professor, *Velocipeden, Automobilen och Motorcykeln*, Stockholm, undated (circa 1930)

Illich, Ivan, *Energy and Equity*, Calder and Boyars, London, 1973

Jackson, Holbrook, *The 1890s*, Penguin, 1950

Jarry, Alfred, *The Supermale*, Cape, London, 1968

Jerome, Jerome K, *My Life and Times*, John Murray, London, 1983

Kobayashi, Keizo, *Pour une Bibliographie du Cyclisme*, Féderation Française du Cyclotourisme, Paris, 1984

Kron, Karl, *Ten Thousand Miles on a Bicycle*, New York, 1887

Laget, Serge, *Le Cyclisme*, Jadault, Courlay (France), 1978

Lange, Annemarie, *Das Wilhelminische Berlin*, East Berlin, 1967

Light Dragoon, A, *Wheels and Woes*, London, undated, 1870 or 1871

Lightwood, J. T., *The Romance of the Cyclists' Touring Club*, CTC, London, 1928

Lockert, Louis, *Vélocipèdes*, Touring-Club de France, Paris, 1896

McClure, S. S., *My Autobiography*, John Murray, London, 1914

McGonagle, Seamus, *The Bicycle in Life, Love, War and Literature*, Pelham, London, 1968

McKenzie, Jean, ed., *Cycling* (extracts from literature), Oxford Univ. Press, 1981

Marinoni, Augusto, *Leonardo da Vinci: L'Automobile e la Bicicletta*, Arcadia Edizioni, Milan, 1981

Marinoni, Augusto, et al., *Laboratorio su Leonardo*, IBM Italy, Milan, 1983

Moffatt, F. C., *Turnpike Road to Tartan Track. The Story of Northern Foot Handicaps*, privately published, Morpeth (UK), 1979

Moxham, S. M., *Fifty Years of Road Racing. A History of the North Road Cycling Club*, Diemer and Reynold, London, 1935

Nicholson, Geoffrey, *The Great Bike Race*, Magnum, London, 1978

Open University Course Team, *Design Processes and Products. Bicycles: Invention and Innovation*, Open University, Milton Keynes (UK), 1983

Perry, P. J., 'Working Class Isolation and Mobility in Rural Dorset, 1837–1936: A Study of Marriage Distances', *Institute of British Geographers, Transactions*, no. 46, March 1969, pp. 121–41.

Pinkerton, John, *At Your Service. A Look at Carrier Cycles*, Pinkerton Press, Birmingham, 1983

Plath, Helmut, *Laufrad–Vélocipède–Hobbyhorse, Eine typologische Unter-suchung*, Festschrift for Wilhelm Hansen, Münster, 1978

Plowden, Stephen and Hillman, Mayer, *The Needless Scourge*, Policy Studies Institute, London, 1984

Plowden, William, *The Motor Car and Politics, 1896–1970*, Bodley Head, London, 1971

Pratt, Charles, *The American Bicycler*, Cambridge Mass., 1879

Priestley, J. B., *English Journey*, 1934; Heinemann reprint: London, 1984

Prynn, David, 'The Clarion Clubs, Rambling and Holiday Associations in Britain since the 1890s', *Journal of Contemporary History*, July 1976, pp. 65–77

Rauck, Volke and Paturi, *Mit dem Rad durch zwei Jahrhunderte*, AT Verlag, Stuttgart, 1984

Rennert, Jack, *One Hundred Years of Bicycle Posters*, Harper and Row, New York, 1973

Reich, Charles A., *The Greening of America*, Penguin (UK), 1972

Replonge, M. A., *Bicycles and Public Transportation*, Rodale Press, Emmaus (US), 1983

Ritchie, Andrew, *King of the Road. An Illustrated History of Cycling*, Wildwood House, London, 1975

Rubenstein, David, 'Cycling in the 1890s', *Victorian Studies*, Autumn 1977

Saunier, Baudry de, *Les Mémoires de Terront*, 1893, reprinted by Prosport, Paris, 1980

Schiefferdecker, Dr med., *Das Radfahren und seine Hygiene*, Stuttgart, 1900; reprinted by Rowohlt, Hamburg, as *Fahrradkultur 1* (edited by H. E. Lessing)

Shattuck, Roger, *The Banquet Years*, Cape, London, 1962

Sinclair, Helen, *Cycle-Clips. A History of Cycling in the North East*, Tyne and Wear County Council Museums, Newcastle upon Tyne, 1985

Sinker, R., *Memorials of Ion Keith-Falconer*, Deighton, Bell, Cambridge, 1888

Smith, Robert, *The Social History of Cycling*, American Heritage Press, New York, 1972

Street, Roger T. C., *Victorian High-Wheelers. The Social Life of the Bicycle where Dorset meets Hampshire*, Dorset Publishing Co., Sherborne, 1979

Terront (see *Saunier, Baudry de*)

Tobin, Gary A., 'The Bicycle Boom of the 1890s', *Journal of Popular Culture*, 7, Spring 1974, pp. 838–849

Velox, *Velocipedes, Bicycles and Tricycles*, Routledge, 1869. Reprinted by S. R. Press, Wakefield (UK), 1971

Vries, Leonard de, *De dolle entree van Automobiel en Velocipee*, de Haan, Bussum (Netherlands), 1973

Waldman, J. R., 'Cycling in Towns: a Quantitive Investigation', LRT1 Working Paper 3, Dept. of Transport, 1977

Walvin, James, *Leisure and Society, 1830 to 1950*, Longmans, London, 1978

Watson, R. and Gray, M., *The Penguin Book of the Bicycle*, Penguin, Harmondsworth (UK), 1978

Weber, Eugen, 'Gymnastics and Sport in Fin-de-Siècle France: Opium of the Classes?' *American History Review*, vol. 76, part 1 1971, pp. 70–98

Wells, H. G., *Experiment in Autobiography*, Gollancz, Cresset, London, 1934; reprinted 1966

Wells, H. G., *The Wheels of Chance*, Dent, London, 1896; reprinted 1984

Wingfield, Walter, *Bicycle Gymkhana and Musical Rides*, London, 1896

Wolf, Wilhelm, *Fahrrad und Radfahrer*, Leipzig, 1890; reprinted in 1979 by Die bibliophilen Taschenbücher, Dortmund.
Woodforde, John, *The Story of the Bicycle*, Routledge and Kegan Paul, London, 1970
Zammattio, Carlo, *Leonardo the Scientist*, Hutchinson, London, 1981

Organisations which specialise in the history of cycling are:

The Veteran-Cycle Club
Susan Duxbury,
42, Parkside Ave.,
Winterbourne,
Bristol,
BS17 1LX
UK

The Wheelmen
Marge Fuehrer,
1708, School House Lane,
Ambler,
Pennsylvania,
19002,
USA

SOURCES OF ILLUSTRATIONS

7   Germanisches National-Museum, Nuremberg
9   Historisches Museum, Vienna
13   Trustees of the British Museum
15   Dover Museum
18   Austrian National Library, Vienna
23, 24, 26, 30, 31, 43, 59, 70, 87, 94, 100, 101, 107, 121   Cyclists' Touring Club, Godalming
28   Allen White
32   Monkwearmouth Station Museum, Sunderland
38, 67   ANWB, The Hague
42, 104   Smithsonian Institution, Washington
44, 56, 85, 88   Beamish North of England Open Air Museum
45, 99, 106   BBC Hulton Picture Library
46   East Sussex County Library
47   Folkestone Central Library
49, 63, 74   Slide Centre, Ilminster

50, 97   Post Office Archive Department
52   North Yorkshire Library
53, 82   University of Oslo Library
54   Gloucester Library
66   Dorothy Couzens
73   Newcastle City Library
75   Mary Evans Picture Library
77   Serge Laget
81   The Royal Library, Copenhagen
86, 92   Manchester Studies Archives
95, 96   *Cycling*
108   Moulton Cycles
109   Richard Francis
110, 113   John Worallo
111   Tim Leighton-Boyce
112   Mike West
114   Borin van Loon
116   Deutsche Presse-Agentur
120   David Nelson
123, 124   Trevor Fishlock
125   John Lowe

INDEX